The Seagull Sartre Library

The Seagull Sartre Library

The Seagull Sartre Library

VOLUME 5
ON MERLEAU-PONTY

JEAN-PAUL SARTRE

TRANSLATED BY
CHRIS TURNER

LONDON NEW YORK CALCUTTA

This work is published with the support of
Institut français en Inde – Embassy of France in India

Seagull Books, 2021

Originally published in Jean-Paul Sartre,
Situations IV © Éditions Gallimard, Paris, 1964

This essay was first published in English translation
by Seagull Books in *Portraits*, 2009

English translation © Christ Turner, 2009, 2010

ISBN 978 0 8574 2 908 7

Typeset by Seagull Books, Calcutta, India
Printed and bound in the USA by Integrated Books International

CONTENTS

＊

MERLEAU-PONTY

How many friends I have lost who are still alive. It was nobody's fault: sometimes it was them, sometimes me. Events made us and brought us together; they also separated us. And Merleau-Ponty, I know, said just this when he happened to think of the people who had been part of his life and left it. Yet he never lost me, and he has had to die for me to lose him. We were equals, friends, but we were not alike; we had understood this immediately and our differences amused us at first. And then, around 1950, the barometer plummeted: a stiff breeze blew through Europe and the world; the swell it whipped up knocked us against each other, then a moment later tossed us to opposite poles. Though so often strained, the ties between us were never severed: if you ask me why, I must say we had a lot of luck and, sometimes, a degree of merit. We each tried to remain true to ourselves and loyal to the other, and we more or less succeeded. Merleau is still too alive for it to be possible to paint his portrait;

it will be easier to achieve a likeness—perhaps unconsciously—if I tell the story of that quarrel that never took place: our friendship.

At the École normale, we knew each other without being part of the same set. He lived outside the college and I was a boarder: each of these two groups regarded themselves as an elite and the others as mere footsloggers. Then came military service: I was a private, he became a second lieutenant: two different orders again.[1] We fell out of touch with each other. He had a chair at Beauvais, I think; I taught at Le Havre. Yet, without knowing it, we were preparing to meet: each of us was trying to understand the world as best he could with the resources at hand. And we had the same resources—which were then called Husserl and Heidegger—because we were part of the same world.

One day in 1947 Merleau told me he had never got over a peerless childhood: it was a time of the cosiest happiness, and only age drove him out of it. Being from adolescence a Pascalian, even before reading Pascal, he experienced his singular selfhood as the singularity of an adventure: a person is something that happens and fades, though not without tracing out the lines of a future ever

---

1 I do not know whether, in 1939, on contact with those whom their leaders refer to curiously as 'men', he regretted leaving the condition of simple soldier. But when I saw my officers, those incompetents, I regretted my pre-war anarchism: since we had to fight, we had been wrong to leave command in the hands of those vain imbeciles. We know that, after the brief interim Resistance period, it remained in their hands; this in some measure explains our misfortunes.

new and ever renewed. What was his life but a lost paradise? An amazing piece of undeserved good luck—a free gift—turned, after the Fall, into adversity; it depopulated the world and disenchanted it in advance. The story is an extraordinary one and yet it is common: our capacity for happiness depends on a particular balance between what our childhood has granted and denied us. If we are entirely deprived or entirely satisfied, we are doomed. The lots that fall to us are infinite in number: it was his lot to have won in life too early. Yet he had to live: it remained for him to make himself, until the end, as events had made him. As they had made him and different: seeking the golden age. His archaic simplicity, crafting from that golden age his myths and what he has since termed his 'style of life', set up preferences —both for traditions, which recall the ceremonies of childhood, and for the 'spontaneity' that evokes its superintended freedom—discovered the meaning of what is happening from what *has happened* and, lastly, turned inventory and acknowledged fact into prophecy. This is what he felt as a young man, without being able to express it yet; these are the byways by which he came to philosophy. He felt a sense of wonderment and that is all there is to it: everything is played out in advance and yet you carry on; why? Why lead a life discredited by absences? And what is it to live?

Our masters, serious and ineffectual, knew nothing of history: they took the view that such questions should not be asked, they were badly framed or—as a stock response of the time had it—'the answers were in the questions'. To think is to measure, said one of them, who did neither. And all of them argued that man and nature can be treated in terms of universal concepts. This was precisely what Merleau-Ponty couldn't accept: tormented by the archaic secrets of his pre-history, he felt irritation at these well-meaning souls who saw themselves as bees and whose philosophy soared above the earth, forgetting that we are bogged down in it from birth. They pride themselves, he was later to say, on looking the world in the face: are they not aware that it envelops and produces us? The most penetrating mind bears the mark of this and one cannot form a single thought that is not deeply conditioned, from the outset, by that Being about which it claims to speak. Since we are each of us ambiguous histories—good and bad fortune, reason and unreason—the origin of which never lies in knowing but in events, it isn't even imaginable that we could express our lives, these unravelling stitches, in terms of knowledge. And what can be the value of human thinking about human beings, since the human being himself is both making the judgement and vouching for it? This was how Merleau 'ruminated on his life'. But the comparison with Kierkegaard is not apposite here: it is too early for that. The Dane was thoroughly averse to Hegelian knowledge; he invented opacities for himself out of a horror of transparency: if the light passed through him, Søren would be done for. With Merleau-Ponty, it was precisely the opposite: he wanted to understand, to understand *himself*; it wasn't his fault if he discovered in practice that universalist idealism was incompatible with what he would call his 'primordial historicity'. He never claimed to grant unreason precedence over rationalism: he merely wanted to bring history into play against the immobilism of the Kantian subject. It was, as Rouletabille said, coming at reason from the right end and nothing more.[2] In short, he was looking for his 'point of anchorage'. We can see what he lacked for beginning at the beginning: 'intentionality', 'situation' and twenty other tools that were to be had in Germany. Around this time I, for quite other reasons, had need of the same instruments. I came to phenomenology through Levinas and went off to Berlin where I stayed for almost a year. When I came back, we were both, without realizing it, at the same point; until September 1939, we went on with our reading and research; at the same pace, but separately.

Philosophy, as is well-known, has no direct efficacy: it took the war to bring us together. In 1941, groups of intellectuals formed all over France, aspiring to resist the victorious enemy. I belonged to one of them, 'Socialism and Liberty'. Merleau joined us. Our meeting again was no chance matter: being each of us a product of the Republican petty-bourgeoisie, our tastes, tradition and

---

2 Joseph Rouletabille was a fictional detective created by Gaston Leroux, now perhaps better known as the author of *The Phantom of the Opera*. [Trans.]

professional consciousness prompted us to defend the freedom of the writer. It was through this freedom that we discovered all the others. Apart from this, we were innocents. Born in enthusiasm, our little unit caught a fever and died a year later, for want of knowing what to do. The other groups in the occupied zone met the same fate, doubtless for the same reason: by 1942, none was left. A little later, Gaullism and the Front National swept up these early resistance fighters. As for the two of us, despite our failure, 'Socialism and Liberty' had brought us together. The times helped us too: there was an unforgettable openness of heart between Frenchmen, which was the reverse side of hatred. By way of this national friendship, which liked everything about everybody from the outset so long as they hated the Nazis, we recognized each other; the essential words were spoken: phenomenology, existence; we discovered our real concerns. Being too individualistic to pool our research, we developed a reciprocity, while remaining separate. Left to ourselves, each of us would have persuaded himself too easily that he had understood the phenomenological idea; together, we embodied its ambiguousness for each other: this was because each of us regarded the alien—and sometimes hostile—labours the other was engaged in as an unexpected deviation from his own work. Husserl became at once the distance between us and the foundation of our friendship. On that terrain, we were, as Merleau, writing about language, has rightly put it: 'differences without terms or, rather, terms engendered by the differences which appear among them.'[3] He retained a nuanced recollection of our talks. Ultimately, he merely wanted to deepen his own understanding and discussions distracted him. And then I made too many concessions to him, and too hastily: he criticized me for this later, in the dark times, and for having exposed *our* viewpoint to third parties without taking account of *his* reservations; he told me he attributed this to pride, to some kind of contempt for others. Nothing can be more unjust: I have always taken the view, and take the view now, that Truth is one and indivisible; on the points of detail it seemed to me then that I had to abandon my views if I had not been able to convince my interlocutor to abandon his or hers. Merleau-Ponty, by contrast, found security in the multiplicity of perspectives: he saw in it the facets of Being. As for remaining silent about his reservations, if I did so it was in good faith. Or almost: does one ever know? My fault was, rather, to drop the decimals so as to achieve unanimity more quickly. In any event, he was not too displeased with me, as he retained the thoroughly amicable idea that I was a reconciler. I do not know if he derived any benefit from these discussions: sometimes I doubt it. But I cannot forget what I owe to them: a thinking that had been aired. In my opinion, this was the purest moment of our friendship.

---

3 See Maurice Merleau-Ponty, *Signs* (Richard McCleary trans.) (Evanston: Northwestern University Press, 1964), p. 39 [*Signes* (Paris: Gallimard, 1960)]. Sartre is paraphrasing slightly. [Trans.]

Yet he did not tell me everything. We no longer spoke about politics except to comment on the news on the BBC. I had lapsed into a distaste for politics which I did not overcome until I was able to join up with a well-established organization. Merleau, formerly more reserved about our joint venture, was slower to forget it: it offered him in miniature the image of an event: it transported the human being back to what he was—to the accident that he was and continued to be, the accident he produced. What had they been through, what had they wanted and, in the end, what had they done, those teachers (including ourselves), students and engineers, suddenly thrown together and just as suddenly separated by a whirlwind?

Merleau-Ponty was, at the time, enquiring into perception; it was, he thought, one of the beginnings of the beginning: this ambiguous testing-out yields up our body by way of the world and the world by way of our body; it is the pivot and the *point of anchorage*. But the world is also history; perhaps we are historical first. In the margins of the book he was slowly writing, he reflected on what, ten years later, seemed to him the fundamental anchoring point. *Phenomenology of Perception*[4] bears the marks of these ambiguous meditations, but I was not able to recognize them; it took him ten years to get to what he had been seeking since adolescence, this

---

4 Maurice Merleau-Ponty, *Phénoménologie de la Perception* (Paris: Gallimard, 1945); *Phenomenology of Perception* (Colin Smith trans.) (London: Routledge and Kegan Paul Ltd, 1962). [Trans.]

being-event of human beings, which we may also term existence. Should I say that phenomenology remained a 'static' in his thesis and that he was going to transform it gradually into a 'dynamic' by a deepening, of which *Humanism and Terror*[5] represented the first stage? This would not be wrong; exaggerated, no doubt, but clear. Let us say that this magnification at least enables us to glimpse the movement of his thought: gently, cautiously, inflexibly, it turned round on itself to reach back, through itself, to the original. In these years preceding the Liberation he had not got far: he knew already, however, that History cannot, any more than Nature, be looked straight in the face. The fact is that it envelops us. How? How did it envelop us, the totality of future time and time past? How were we to discover the others in ourselves as our deep truth? How were we to perceive ourselves in them as the rule of their truth? The question already arises at the level of perceptual spontaneity and 'intersubjectivity'; it becomes more concrete and urgent when we resituate the historical agent within the universal flow. Our labours and travails, our tools, government, customs and traditions—how were persons to be 'inserted' into this? Conversely, how could they be extracted from a web they were constantly spinning and that was, in its turn, constantly producing them?

---

5 Maurice Merleau-Ponty, *Humanisme et terreur, essai sur le problème communiste* (Paris: Gallimard, 1947); *Humanism and Terror: An Essay on the Communist Problem* (John O'Neill trans.) (Boston: Beacon Press, 1969). [Trans.]

Merleau had expected to make a peacetime living; a war had made him into a warrior and he, for his part, had made war. What if this strange whirligig marked the scope and limits of historical action? He had to look closely into this. As investigator, witness, defendant and judge, he went back and, in the light of our defeat and of the future German defeat—of which, after Stalingrad we felt assured—examined the false war he had fought, the false peace he had thought he was living through, and himself, as ever, at the pivot of these things, the biter bit, the mystifier mystified, both victim and accomplice, despite a good faith that was not in doubt and yet had, nonetheless, to be questioned.[6] All this went on in silence: he had no need of a partner to cast this new light on the singularity of his times, on his own singularity. But we have the evidence that he was constantly reflecting on his times; as early as 1945 he wrote: 'When all is said and done, we have learned history and it is our contention that we must not forget it.'[7]

This was a courtesy 'we': it would take me a good few years yet to learn what he knew. Having known deep satisfaction from birth, then frustration, he was destined, by his experience, to discover the force of circumstance, the inhuman powers that steal our acts and thoughts

6 Not, as I did in 1942, by an eidetics of bad faith, but by the empirical study of our historical allegiances and the inhuman forces perverting them.

7 Maurice Merleau-Ponty, 'La guerre a eu lieu,' *Les Temps modernes*, 1 (October 1945).

from us. As a man invested with a role and yet encircled, a man predestined but free, his original intuition disposed him to understand *the event*, that adventure that comes out of everywhere and nowhere, with no consistency or signification until it has filled us with its hazardous shades, until it has forced us to grant its iron necessity freely and in spite of ourselves. And then he suffered from his relations with others: everything had been too good too quickly; the Nature that at first enveloped him was the Mother Goddess, his mother, whose eyes bestowed upon him what he saw; she was the *alter ego*; by her and in her he lived that 'intersubjectivity of immanence' he has often described and which causes us to discover our 'spontaneity' through another. With childhood dead, love remained, just as strong, but disconsolate. Being sure that he could never recover the lost intimacy, he didn't know what to ask of his friends: everything and nothing; at times too much, at others not enough. He moved quickly from demands to lack of interest, not without suffering from these failures which confirmed his exile. Misunderstandings, estrangements, separations with wrong on both sides: private life had already taught him that our acts register themselves in our little world in a manner different from what we had wished, making us other than we were by retrospectively lending us intentions we did not have but will have had from now on. After 1939 he saw these errors of reckoning, these unnecessary expenses that must be accepted because one has failed to foresee them, as the very characteristics of historical action. In 1945 he wrote, 'We have been led to accept and regard as our own not only our intentions, the meanings our acts have for us, but also the consequences of those acts externally, the meaning they assume in a certain historical context.'[8] He saw 'his shadow cast on history as on a wall, that form which his actions assumed for the outside world, that objective Spirit that was himself.'[9] Merleau felt sufficiently engaged to have constantly a sense of restoring the world to the world, sufficiently free to objectivize himself in history by that restitution. He was happy to compare himself to a wave: one crest among others, with the whole of a head sea holding in a hem of foam. As a mix of strange chance occurrences and generalities, historical man appears when his act, performed and planned remotely, to the point of the most alien objectivity, introduces the beginnings of reason into the original irrationality. To his adversaries, Merleau replied, in all certainty, that his feeling for existence did not set him in opposition to Marxism and, in actual fact, the well-known saying, 'Men make history, but not in circumstances of their own choosing' could pass, in his eyes, for a Marxist version of his own thinking.

The Communist intellectuals made no mistake on this point. As soon as the lull of 1945 was over, they attacked me: my political thinking was confused, my

8 Merleau-Ponty, 'La guerre a eu lieu'.
9 Merleau-Ponty, 'La guerre a eu lieu'.

ideas could do harm. Merleau, by contrast, seemed close
to them. A flirtation began: Merleau-Ponty often saw
Courtade, Hervé and Desanti;[10] his traditionalism found
solace in their company: after all, the Communist Party
is a tradition. He preferred its rites, its thought baked
and hardened by twenty-five years of history, to the spec-
ulations of those who belonged to no party.

He was not, however, a Marxist: he did not reject the
Marxist idea, but he rejected Marxism as dogma. He did
not accept that historical materialism was the sole light
of history, nor that that light emanates from an eternal
source which stands, in principle, outside the vicissitudes
of historical events. He criticized this objectivistic intellectualism, like classical rationalism, for looking the world
in the face and forgetting that in fact it enwraps us. He
would have accepted the doctrine if he could have seen
it merely as a net cast upon the sea, unfurled and refurled
by the swell, its truth dependent, precisely, on its perpetual
participation in the sea's endless commotion. He could see
it as a system of reference, but, on condition that, in referring to it, we change it; he could see it as an explanation,
on condition that it change shape as it explain. Should we
speak of 'Marxist relativism'? Yes and no. Whatever the
doctrine, he mistrusted it, fearing he might find it to be
a construction of that philosophy that 'soars above the
earth'. A relativism, then, but a precautionary relativism;

---

10 Pierre Courtade (1915–63), Pierre Hervé (1913–93) and Jean-
Toussaint Desanti (1914–2002). [Trans.]

he believed in just the one absolute: our point of anchorage, life. What, then, ultimately was his criticism of the Marxist theory of history? Crucially this and nothing else: it allowed no room for contingency:

> Every historical undertaking has something of an adventure about it, being never guaranteed by any *absolutely* rational structure of things. It always involves a utilization of chance, one has always to be crafty with things (and with people) since one has to extract from them an order that was not given with them. The possibility of an enormous compromise remains, of a corruption of history in which the class struggle, which is powerful enough to destroy, would not be powerful enough to build, and in which the broad outlines of history as mapped out in the *Communist Manifesto* would fade away.[11]

The contingency of each and all, the contingency of the human adventure; within this, the contingency of the Marxist adventure—we come back to Merleau-Ponty's fundamental experience. He had first reflected on the singularity of his life, then, moving on to contemplate his historical existence, he had discovered they were both cut from the same cloth.

---

11 Sartre provides no references for these quotations, but this passage can be found in Merleau-Ponty, *Sens et non-sens* (Paris: Gallimard, 1996), pp. 201–02. [Trans.]

With these reservations, he accepted historical materialism as a grid, as a regulative idea or, if one prefers, as a heuristic schema:

> There have been enough writers in the last fifteen years who have falsely gone beyond Marxism for us to take care to distinguish ourselves from them. To go beyond a doctrine, you have first to have come up to its level and you have to explain what it explains better than it does itself. If we raise some questions with regard to Marxism, this is not to prefer a conservative philosophy of history that would be even more abstract.

In short, he was a Marxist for want of anything better.

Let us be clear about this: Marxism is basically a practice that has its origins in class struggle. Deny that struggle and nothing remains. In 1945—and so long as the Communist Party shared power with the bourgeois parties—that struggle was not clearly decipherable. The Party's young intellectuals believed in it devoutly. They were not wrong; I say they *believed* in it because they could not *see* it behind the deceptive mask of national unity. Merleau-Ponty often irritated them because he only half believed in it. He had reflected on the consequences of victory: no more allies, two giants face to face. These latter, concerned to avoid friction, had recast the globe at Yalta: I'll have the sunset lands, you have the sunrise; for peace they had little concern; it was beyond doubt that there would be a Third World War; each of the two, anxious to win it as soon as possible, came to an arrangement with the other, to postpone it until such time as they had acquired the better positions. The balance of forces remained, however, temporarily in favour of the West: hence, in that moment of history, revolution became impossible in Europe; neither Churchill nor Roosevelt, nor in the end Stalin, would have tolerated it. We know what happened to the Greek resistance and how it was liquidated. Everything is clear today: the whole earth became united in a single history; there ensued this contradiction, indecipherable at the time, that the class struggle transformed itself in places into conflicts between nations—hence into deferred wars. Today the Third World shows us the truth of this; in 1945, we could neither understand the change that had taken place nor accept it. In short, we were blind; Merleau-Ponty, who had one good eye, came to conclusions that were astonishing because they seemed inevitable: if the revolution can be halted from outside by the concern to preserve the international balance, if external forces can nip it in the bud, if the workers must look not to themselves but to a planetary conflict for their emancipation, then the revolutionary class has gone on leave. The bourgeoisie continued to exist, surrounded by the immense mass of workers it exploited and atomized. But the proletariat, that invincible force that passed sentence on capitalism and whose mission was to overturn it, was out to lunch. It was quite possible that it would return; perhaps tomorrow, perhaps in half a century; it may, also, never return. Merleau-Ponty registered this absence, deplored it as seemed fitting and proposed that we organize immediately just in case it should continue. He went so far as to outline a programme in a text which I quote from memory, though I'm certain I do so quite accurately: 'In the meantime, let us undertake to do nothing that might prevent the rebirth of the proletariat; better, we should do all we can to help it to reconstitute itself; in short, we should follow Communist Party policy.' I can, at any rate, vouch for these last words, as I was so struck by them: born out of the class struggle, the Communist Party developed its policy as a function of that struggle; in the capitalist countries, it would not survive the disappearance of the proletariat. Now, Merleau-Ponty no longer believed in civil war, contesting by that very token the legitimacy of Communist organization: the paradox is that he proposed, at the same moment, that we should align ourselves with the Party.

There was another paradox. Go and find a bishop and, just as an experiment, tell him: 'God is dead, I doubt he'll revive but, in the meantime, I'm with you.' You will be thanked for your kind offer, but it will not be possible to accept it. Now, Merleau's Communist friends had taken the opposite stance: they said some harsh things to him in polite terms, but they didn't reject him. Thinking about it, this is no surprise. The Party had come out on top from the Resistance: it was less strict about the choice of its fellow travellers. Above all, its intellectuals were uneasy about their lives: being radical by their position, they would have liked the proletariat to set about gaining new ground, to resume its forward march; the bourgeoisie, terrorized by the publicity given to its betrayals, would have put up no opposition. Instead of this, action was postponed. They said, 'Let's seize power' and the reply came back: the British and Americans would land within the hour. A new contradiction appeared within the movement for political advance since, to save peace and the socialist countries, a revolution demanded from the inside by the masses could be countermanded from the outside. These young people who had come to the Party through the Resistance, did not lose their trust in it; but there were doubts and frictions. After all, France was a bourgeois democracy; what was the Communist Party doing in the tripartite government? Was it not a hostage to capital? They faithfully transmitted the slogans that troubled them: 'you have to know how to end a strike' and 'the reconstruction of the country is the revolutionary objective'. But they couldn't stop Merleau's conclusions worrying them a little. At the edges. After all, he approved of the Party's reformist policy, that policy of which they themselves, out of sheer obedience, were the agents. Could they blame him for repeating out loud what they sometimes said under their breath: where is the proletariat? In actual fact, it was there. But bridled and muzzled.

And by whom? They became irritated a little more each day by Merleau-Ponty, that Cassandra; Merleau-Ponty became irritated with them—each as wrongly as the other.

Merleau misunderstood the rootedness of his friends. He returned to the question fifteen years later, in the preface to *Signs*. There, by contrast, he stresses the status of the party activist who is embedded and entrusted with a mission and who must, nonetheless, contribute by his allegiances and actions to making the party that makes him. It is an ambiguous expression of regret, which leads him, above all, to justify resignations from the Party: it is all very well to have fun judging a policy calmly and serenely from the outside. When those who produce that policy on a day-to-day basis, if only through their acquiescence, discover its meaning, and when they see their shadows cast on the wall, they have no alternative but to break with it. But the argument can be turned around and I believe he knew it: for all these young people of 1945, floundering about between their sincerely held beliefs and their sworn allegiance, by way of actions they assumed daily and whose meaning they saw change in their hands, on more than one occasion the thinker 'soaring' above the fray was Merleau-Ponty.

His friends were mistaken about him in their turn: they did not know the path he had followed. From some conversations we had later, I was left with the feeling that he had been closer to Marxism before 1939 than he ever was afterwards. What distanced him from it? I imagine it was the trials; the fact that he spoke about them at such length in *Humanism and Terror* shows that he continued to be very affected by them. After that, the Nazi-Soviet Pact made little impression on him: he amused himself by writing rather 'Machiavellian' letters to 'apportion roles'. Friends and the writings of Rosa Luxemburg had converted him to the idea of that 'spontaneity of the masses' that saw the general movement as being closely related to its particular form; when he saw Reason of State gleaming out from behind it, he turned away.

He had been a Christian at twenty but ceased to be so because, as he said, 'You believe you believe, but you don't believe.' More exactly, he wanted Catholicism to reintegrate him into the unity of immanence and that was precisely what it couldn't do: Christians love each other in God. I shall not say that he went straight from there to socialism: that would be too schematic. But there came a time when he encountered Marxism and asked what it had to offer: he concluded that it offered the future unity of a classless society and, in the meantime, a warm friendship in struggle. After 1936, there can be no doubt: it was the Party that troubled him. One of his most constant characteristics was to seek the lost immanence everywhere, to be thrown back by that immanence itself towards some transcendent entity and thereupon to take his leave. Yet he did not remain at this level of the original contradiction: between 1950 and 1960, he gradually conceived a new connection between being and inter- subjectivity; but in 1945, though he dreamed perhaps of going beyond it, he had found no way to do so.

In short, he had been through a great deal when, despite the feelings of revulsion he had at times experienced, he proposed his severe, disillusioned, *attentiste* Marxism. And it was true that he had 'learned history' without having any taste for it, from his vocation and out of obstinacy. It was true, too, that he was never again to forget it. This is something his Communist friends did not see at the time, tending, as they did, more towards unconditional commitments than precise, limited agreements. For his part, being concerned only with deepening his relation to history, he would have offered no purchase for their criticisms, I imagine, and would have remained stubbornly silent, if we had not, by chance, founded *Les Temps modernes*. He now possessed the instrument of expression and was virtually compelled to express the detail of his thinking.

We had dreamed of having the review since 1943. If the Truth is indivisible, I thought, then we must, as Gide said of God, seek it 'only everywhere'. Every social product, every attitude—the most private and the most public—are allusive embodiments of it. An anecdote reflects an age as effectively as a political Constitution. We would be seekers after meaning; we would speak the truth about the world and our lives. Merleau thought me over-optimistic: was I sure there was meaning everywhere? To which I might have replied that the meaning of non-meaning exists and it was up to us to find it. And I know what he would have replied in turn: cast as much light on barbarism as you will, you will not dispel its obscurity. The discussion never took place: I was more dogmatic, he was more nuanced, but that is a matter of temperament or, as they say, of character. We had a single desire: to get out of the tunnel, to see things clearly. He wrote: 'Our only recourse lies in a reading of the present that is as complete and faithful as possible; a reading that does not prejudge its meaning and even recognizes its chaos and non-meaning where they are to be found, but is not averse to discerning a direction and an idea in that present, where they exist.'[12]

This was our programme. Today, after Merleau's death, it is still the programme of the review. We would have to say that the real difference was our inequality. After he had learned history, I was no longer his equal. I was still stuck in the questioning of facts while he was already attempting to make events speak.

Facts *repeat* themselves. They are, of course, always new—but what of it? The annual play by the boulevard playwright is new. He had to come up with the idea and then he thought about it and worked on it; every speech was a stroke of inspiration, and the actors in their turn

---

12 Merleau-Ponty, *Sens et non-sens*, p. 205. [Trans.]

had to 'get inside' the piece. For days they said 'I don't feel the part' and then, suddenly, 'I feel it.' And in the end, on the day of the dress rehearsal, the unexpected happens: the play became what it was—namely, just the same as all the others. Facts confirm and begin anew: they reveal customs, old contradictions and sometimes, more deeply, structures. The same adultery has been committed for fifty years, every evening, before the same bourgeois audience in the heart of Paris. By looking only for permanencies of this kind, I was hoping unconsciously that we would become the ethnographers of French society.

Merleau-Ponty didn't hate these permanencies. Indeed, he loved the child-like return of seasons and ceremonies. But for this very reason, pining hopelessly for his childhood, he knew it would not return. It would be something too wonderful if, in the world of adults, the adult could be visited by the grace of his earliest years: life would be too perfect. Merleau, the exile, had *felt* at an early stage what I could only *know*: you cannot go back; you cannot take a second turn; by its irreversibility, the sweet contingency of birth transforms itself into a destiny. I was not unaware that you descend life's course and never reverse its direction; but, duped by the bourgeois myth of progress, I cherished for a long time the illusion that I was a little better each day. Progress: the accumulation of capital and virtue; you keep everything. In short, I was approaching excellence; it was the masking of death, which today stands naked. He was moving away from it: being born to die, nothing could restore the immortality of his earliest years; this was his original experience of *the event*.

In the middle of the last century, he would have lived time backwards, though in vain, as Baudelaire did after the '*fêlure*': the golden age is past; there is room now only for decline. It is to Merleau's credit that he avoided this reactionary myth: let there be as much decline as you will, but it is our decline, we cannot suffer it without creating it or, in other words, without producing man and his works through that decline. The event swoops on us like a thief and throws us into a ditch or hoists us up on to a wall; dazed, we see nothing. Yet hardly has it scarpered away than we find ourselves so deeply changed that we no longer even understand how we could love, live and act before. Who in 1945 would have remembered the 1930s? They were preparing quietly for retirement; the Occupation had killed them off; only bones remained. Some still dreamed of a return to pre-war days. Merleau knew it would not happen and it was criminal and futile to wish for it: when he wondered in 1945 whether the human adventure would sink into barbarism or rescue itself through socialism, he was putting the question to universal history as though it were his own life: time lost? time regained? Divergence, deviation, drift—these words from his pen, a hundred times rewritten, attest to the fact that we gain nothing without a loss, that the future, even the nearest, most docile future, betrays our hopes and calculations. But most of the time it betrays them by bringing them to fruition: our past acts come back to us, from the depths of future time, unrecognizable, but nonetheless our own; one either had to despair or find in those acts the changing reason for change and, not being able to restore the old facts, at least establish them in the heart of the event that repudiates them. We would try to govern the strange slippage we call history from within, by seeking, in the movement that carries us along, the implicit objectives of human beings, so as to propose those objectives to these human beings explicitly. This meant questioning the event in its unpredictability—without pre-judging anything—to find a logic of temporality in it. One might be tempted to call that logic 'dialectical' if Merleau had not already objected to that term and had not, ten years later, more or less repudiated it.[13]

All in all, the pre-war period denied time: when a cyclone had blown down our walls, we searched for the survivors among the rubble and told them, 'It's nothing.' The most extraordinary thing is, they believed us. Merleau-Ponty 'learned history' quicker than we did because he took a full and painful pleasure in passing time. This is what made him our political commentator, without his even having wished to be and without anyone even noticing.

---

13 He had not pronounced on this question in 1945: he thought the word too ambitious to apply it to the modest activity of *Les Temps modernes*.

Les Temps modernes had at that point an editorial board that was anything but homogeneous: Jean Paulhan, Raymond Aron and Albert Ollivier were all friends of ours, of course. But, though no one knew this, least of all ourselves,[14] we did not share any of their ideas. In fact, our inert coexistence had been, not so long before, a lively comradeship: some had just come from London, others from underground. But the Resistance fragmented: everyone returned to their natural home, some to *Le Figaro*, others to the RPF, yet others to the *Nouvelle Nouvelle Revue Française*. The Communists themselves, having participated in the first issue in the person of Jean Kanapa, took their leave. This was a heavy blow for those of us who remained: we lacked experience. Merleau saved the review by agreeing to take charge of it: he was editor- in-chief and political editor. This happened naturally. He didn't offer me his services and I didn't take the liberty of 'selecting' him: we both realized, after a certain time, that he was filling these two posts and that he couldn't leave them without the review going under. We discussed only one matter: since the editorial board had disappeared from the cover, I suggested printing Merleau's name there alongside my own: we would have been the two 'directors'. He turned me down flat. I put

---

14 Sartre writes '*nous-même*' here, singular, not '*nous-mêmes*', which suggests an authorial 'we' that refers to himself alone: the context seems to suggest, however, that he is thinking of those who remained at *Les Temps modernes* beyond its first beginnings, i.e. chiefly Merleau and himself. [Trans.]

the same offer to him a hundred times in the ensuing years, always on the simple grounds that it would have been a truer reflection of the actual position. A hundred times, relaxed and smiling, he turned me down again, citing circumstantial reasons, but never the same ones. Since his reasons changed constantly, but his position did not, I concluded that he was concealing his true motives from me. I confronted him with this and he rejected the idea, though with no great vigour: he was not trying to deceive me, but merely wanted to put a stop to the discussion. And then, whatever the subject, he never liked the debate to get to the crux of the matter. On this point, he won: I know no more of his reasons today than I did in 1945. Was it modesty? I doubt it: this wasn't about sharing honours but responsibilities. On the other hand, I have been told, 'At the time you were better known: he was too proud to accept the fruits of that fame.' It is true that I was better known and it was nothing to boast of: it was the time of the *rats de cave*,[15] of existential suicides; the respectable newspapers heaped dirt on me and so did the gutter press: I had fame, but it was born of misconceptions. But those who read *Samedi Soir*'s interesting account of a virgin whom I apparently lured to my room to show her a camembert did not read *Les Temps modernes* and were not even aware of its existence. On the other hand, the real readers of the review knew both of us equally; they had read our

---

15 Literally, 'cellar rats'—those who frequented the jazz-saturated cellar nightclubs of the immediate post-war years. [Trans.]

essays and preferred the one or the other of us, or felt no great preference but no animosity either. Merleau knew this as well as I did: we had received letters and shown them to each other. All in all, his audience and mine—the audience of *Les Temps modernes*—were the same people. And the best people one could wish for, not shooting the pianist, and judging him on his work and not concerning themselves with other matters. From my dubious reputation Merleau could neither suffer nor profit. Was he perhaps afraid of being compromised? Nothing was less like him: he proved this in the review itself, publishing articles that provoked scandal and signing them with his own name. So, what can we say? Why did he stubbornly persist in signing editorials with the letters T. M., when, though I accepted them unreservedly, he had conceived and written every word? All the writings to which he didn't own up were randomly attributed to me: there was some logic to this, since I claimed to be in sole charge. And last year, leafing through some foreign bibliographies, I discovered that I was the author of his article on the Soviet camps—the very one he recognized and legitimized in his last book.[16] Why had he not signed it in 1950, given that he was later to republish it? Why did he republish it ten years later, when he hadn't wanted to sign it? Why create all these 'bastards' for the review when it was wholly within

---

16 Sartre is referring to the article 'The USSR and the Camps', reprinted in *Signs*, pp. 263–73. It was published originally in January 1950. [Trans.]

his power to 'regularize' their status? This is the question; I cannot claim to have an answer. Yet one had to get on with life; I contented myself with the most convenient explanation: he valued his independence and would have felt as a burden any bond but the tacit understanding, renewed with each issue, that committed no one and that either of us could break at a moment's notice. This is a possible explanation, and yet I think today that he mistrusted me: he knew my incompetence, and he feared my zeal; if I should begin talking politics, then where would we be? I have no evidence of this distrust except for the following. In 1947, I published 'What is Literature?' in the review. He read the first proofs and thought he had found in them a sentence which, as was the fashion at the time, equated fascism with 'Stalinism' beneath the common appellation of 'totalitarian regimes'. I was in Italy and he wrote to me immediately; I received the letter in Naples and I remember my stupefaction. It said, more or less: 'If you really apply the same yardsticks to communism and Nazism, then I beg you to accept my resignation.' Fortunately, as I was able to prove to him, it was simply a typographical error. We left matters there. But when I reflect on it, it reveals the extent of his distrust: first, the text, at the proof stage, was incomprehensible and clearly mangled; second, as Merleau knew, I had never indulged in that kind of silliness; last, his resignation was offered rather too eagerly. All in all, it is very clear that he was expecting the worst. But what strikes me most is that his fear was that I would defect to the *Right*. Why? Did he see me as temperamentally right-wing? Or was he simply afraid that the hyena with the fountain pen, frozen out by the jackals, would seek admission to the Pen Club? In any event, he was taking precautions against possible blunders on my part: if one should prove inexcusable, he could be away within twenty-four hours. This emergency exit was still in place five years later when a political disagreement drove us apart: yet Merleau did not use it; so long as he could hope that our contradictions would be overcome, he remained. His letter of 1947 proves he would have left the review there and then if I had let it fall into a Rightist rut. When I moved to the Left, he accepted being compromised: he believed he could already see the ditch and that we would imminently be pitched into it, yet he remained at my side, determined to jump only as a last resort. For a long time I thought he was wrong not to have joined me in the stocks: public collaboration would have forced us, I told myself, to make concessions on both sides; we would have been tactful with each other to save the collegiate editorship. Yet for some time now I have tended to believe he was right: in 1952, our differences could neither be masked nor overcome. They arose not out of our temperaments but from the situation: since the name of Merleau wasn't mentioned, we were able to delay matters a little longer. The secret nature of the bond between us, which had been conceived to make withdrawal easy for him, enabled us to stay together till the last moment. The separation was a quiet one, we had no need to proclaim it or, in other words, to turn it into a publicized quarrel. This is perhaps what saved our friendship.

In our closest circles, all these precautions afforded him the reputation of an *éminence grise*. This was quite wrong, particularly as he was nobody's adviser: master of his sphere, as I was of mine, his role—like mine—was to make decisions and write.

He was, however, extremely keen that I should read his articles, both those which he signed T. M., which spoke in the name of the review, and the others bearing his own name, which committed only himself. Let me be clear here: this attitude *seems like* that of an employee, a functionary having his actions 'covered' by the competent authority. It was, in fact, quite the opposite: Merleau was entirely his own boss. He knew his way around the ambiguous world of politics better than I did and I knew that. It would be an understatement to say I trusted him: it seemed to me that, when I read him, he revealed my own thinking to me. But our gentlemen's agreement demanded that he consult me: writing anonymously, he did not want me to be saddled with his writings. He was as tactful as possible about it: I was still a stammerer in this new language he already spoke and he was not unaware of this. Reluctant either to coerce or inveigle me, he brought me his manuscripts without comment. In the early days, he had to make a lot of effort to be read: the political labyrinth confused me, I approved everything in advance and in haste, and then ran off. He'd find out my hiding place and track me down to it. I'd find him suddenly standing there, smiling and holding out his manuscript: 'I agree,' I'd stammer. 'That's good,' he'd reply, not moving, 'But all the same,' he'd add patiently, indicating with his left hand the sheets of paper in his right, 'you should read these.'

I read and learned, and in the end I was passionate about my reading. He was my guide; it was *Humanism and Terror* that caused me to take the plunge. That little book, so densely written, showed me the method and the object: it gave me the nudge I needed to wrest me from my immobilism. As is well-known, it provoked scandal everywhere. Communists who see no harm in it today loathed it at the time. But, particularly to our Right, it raised a fine hullabaloo. One sentence in particular, which equated opponents with traitors and traitors with opponents, triggered the reaction. In Merleau's mind, this sentence applied to those anxious, threatened societies that huddle together around a revolution. But attempts were made to present it as a sectarian condemnation of any opposition to Stalin. In just a few days, Merleau became the bloodthirsty revolutionary. When Simone de Beauvoir visited them in New York, the editors of the *Partisan Review* made no effort to conceal their disgust: we were being manipulated; it was the hand of Moscow that held the pen of our *père Joseph*.[17] What idiots! One evening, at Boris Vian's, Camus took Merleau to task,

17 Père Joseph—Father Joseph—was the *éminence grise* of Cardinal de Richelieu. [Trans.]

accusing him of justifying the Moscow trials. It was painful: I can still see them, Camus outraged, Merleau-Ponty courteous and firm, a little pale, the one permitting himself, the other forbidding himself, the splendours of violence. Suddenly Camus turned away and left. I ran after him, accompanied by Jacques Bost, and caught up with him in the empty street. I tried as best I could to explain Merleau's thinking, which Merleau himself had not deigned to do. The only result was that we parted on bad terms; it took more than six months and a chance meeting to bring us together again. This is not a pleasant memory for me: what a stupid idea to try to play the peacemaker! I was, admittedly, to the right of Merleau and to the left of Camus; what black humour can have prompted me to play go-between to two friends who were both not long afterwards to criticize my friendship for the Communists, and who are both dead, unreconciled?

In fact, with this little sentence which caused such a violent reaction, but which everyone accepts today as a basic truth with a universal validity beyond the limits set for it by its author, Merleau had done nothing but apply to other circumstances what the war had taught him: we shall not be assessed on our intentions alone. As much as, and more than, the intended effects of our acts, the basis on which we are judged will be the unintended consequences that we have divined and exploited, and for which, in any event, we have assumed responsibility. 'The man of action,' he wrote later, quoting Hegel, 'has the certainty that, through his action, necessity will become contingency and contingency necessity.' In so doing, he was asking the true philosophical question of history: what is a detour and what does it mean to veer off course? We started out in rough weather and a head-wind, we battled on stoically and have grown old in hard times; this, here, is what we have achieved. What remains of the old goals? What has disappeared? A new society has been born along the way, shaped by the undertaking and deflected by its deflection. What can it accept? And what must it reject or risk doing itself a serious mischief? And, whatever the heritage, who can say whether we have travelled the shortest path or whether we must attribute the meanderings to everyone's failings?

Through this rough justice of injustice, in which the bad are saved by their works and men of good faith condemned to hell for acts committed with a pure heart, I finally discovered the reality of the event. In a word, it was Merleau who converted me: at heart I was an anarchist laggard, I saw a chasm between the vague fantasies of collectivities and the precise ethics of my private life. He set me straight: he taught me that this ambiguous undertaking that is both rational and mad, ever unpredictable and always foreseen, attaining its objectives when it forgets them, missing them when it tries to remain loyal to them, destroying itself in the false purity of failure and dissipating itself in victory, abandoning its prime mover on the way or denouncing him when he no longer believes himself responsible for it, was something I found everywhere, both in the most intimate recesses of my life and in the broad daylight of history, and that there is only one undertaking and it is the same for everyone— the event that makes us by becoming action, the action that unmakes us by becoming, through us, event—and, since Hegel and Marx, it bears the name *praxis*. In a word, he revealed to me that I made history in the same way as Monsieur Jourdain made prose. The course of events broke down the last ramparts of my individualism and swept away my private life, and I discovered myself in just those very places where I began to slip beyond my own grasp. I came to know myself: and I was more obscure, in the full light of day, than I believed myself to be, and two billion times richer. The time had come: our age demanded a dissertation on French politics from all men of letters. I prepared myself for that ordeal; Merleau instructed me without teaching, by his experi- ence, by the consequences of his writings. If philosophy is to be, as he said, an 'educative spontaneity', I may say he was for me the philosopher of his politics. As for his politics, it is my claim we could have had no other and that it was appropriate. If one is to last, one must begin well: the beginning came from him and it was excellent. Proof of this is that our readers have taken all the subse- quent twists and turns with us; it will soon be seventeen years since we published the first issue of *Les Temps mod- ernes*; we have regularly gained subscribers and at the very most a few dozen have left us.

It was possible in 1945 to choose between two positions. Two and no more. The first and best was to address ourselves to the Marxists, to them alone and to denounce the way the Revolution had been nipped in the bud, condemn the murder of the Resistance and bemoan the fragmentation of the Left. A number of periodicals adopted this line courageously and disappeared, unheeded; it was the happy time when people had ears so as not to hear and eyes so as not to see. Far from believing that these failures condemned the attempts, I take the view that we could have imitated them without going under: the strength and weakness of these publications was that they confined themselves to the political sphere; ours published novels, literary essays, reportage and non-fiction material: these kept it afloat. However, in order to denounce the betrayal of the Revolution, one had first to be revolutionary: Merleau was not, and I was not yet. We didn't even have the right to declare ourselves Marxist, despite our sympathies for Marx. Now, Revolution is not a vague sentiment: it is a daily practice illuminated by a theory. And, though it is not enough to have read Marx to be a revolutionary, you connect with him sooner or later when you campaign for revolution. The conclusion is clear: only men shaped by that discipline could criticize the Left effectively; at the time, then, they had to belong, in one way or another, to Trotskyist circles; but, without it being at all their fault, that affinity disqualified them: within that mystified Left that dreamt of unity, they were regarded as 'splitters'. Merleau-Ponty saw the threats clearly too; he noted that the working class' forward march was halted and he knew the reasons for it. But if he had shown the workers gagged, chained, mystified and defrauded of their victory, this petty-bourgeois intellectual—even if he had wept hot tears for them, even if he had made his readers weep them—would have been laying the demagogy on thick. When, on the other hand, he concluded that the proletariat had gone on holiday, he was being sincere and true to himself, and I was being true to myself when I backed his conclusions. Revolutionaries, us? Come off it! At the time, Revolution seemed the most likeable of myths, a Kantian idea, so to speak; I repeated the *word* with respect, but I knew nothing of the *thing*. We were moderate intellectuals whom the Resistance had pulled to the Left; but not enough; and then again, the Resistance was dead; left to ourselves, what could we be but reformists?

There remained the other attitude. We had no choice to make; it forced itself upon us. As products of the middle classes, we attempted to form a link between the intellectual petty-bourgeoisie and the Communist intellectuals. That bourgeoisie had engendered us; its culture and values were our heritage; but the Occupation and Marxism had taught us that neither the culture nor the values were to be taken for granted. We called on our friends in the Communist Party to supply us with the requisite tools to wrest humanism from the bourgeoisie. And we asked all our friends on the Left to do the work with us. Merleau wrote: 'We were not wrong in 1939 to want freedom, truth, happiness, and openness between human beings, and we are not renouncing humanism. [But] the war . . . taught us that these values remain nominal . . . without an economic and political infrastructure to bring them into existence.'[18] I can see that this position, which might be termed eclectic, was not viable in the long term, but I can also see that the French and international situations made it the only one possible. Why would we have taken things to extremes? We had, admittedly, forgotten the class struggle but we were not alone in that. Events had chosen us to bear witness to what the petty-bourgeois intelligentsia wanted in 1945, at the moment when the Communists had lost both the means and the intent to overthrow the regime. Paradoxically, that intelligentsia, as it seems to me, wanted the Communist Party to make reformist concessions and the French proletariat to regain its revolutionary aggression. The paradox is merely an apparent one: this chauvinistic class, exasperated by five years of occupation, was afraid of the USSR, but would have come to an accommodation with a 'home-grown' revolution. There are, however, degrees in being and thought: whatever the appeal of this revolutionary, chauvinistic reformism, Merleau did not care for being the herald of a proletariat in

---

18 Maurice Merleau-Ponty, *La guerre a eu lieu* (Paris: Éditions Champ social, 2007), p. 55. This work, originally published in *Les Temps modernes*, 1 (October 1945): 48–66, is also reprinted in *Sens et non-sens*. [Trans.]

French colours. For his part, he had undertaken—as did others in other countries at around this same time—an enormous labour of confrontation: he threw our abstract concepts out to the Marxists, and their Marxism changed, as they assimilated those concepts, into what we know it to be today.

Today, the task is easier: because the Marxists—Communists or otherwise—have taken it up themselves. In 1948, it was very thorny, particularly because the Communist party intellectuals felt no compunction about telling these two suspect, empty-handed bourgeois, who had volunteered themselves as fellow travellers, where to get off. We had to defend Marxist ideology without concealing our reservations and hesitations; to travel with men to whom we expressed our goodwill and who, in return, called us *intellectuels-flics*; to make our ripostes without being insulting or breaking off relations; to criticize, moderately but freely, these hypersensitive souls who could not tolerate any reservations; to assert, despite our solitude, that we were marching at their side, alongside the working class—the bourgeois fell about laughing when they read us—and yet allow ourselves, when necessary, to run ahead of the Party, as we did at the beginning of the war in Indochina; to struggle for peace and détente in our little magazine, as though we were running a mass-market daily; to deny ourselves any righteous passions, particularly self-importance and anger; to speak in the wilderness as though we were addressing the assembled nation and yet not lose sight of our extreme smallness; to remember at every moment that you don't need success to persevere but that the point of persevering is to achieve success. Despite the jibes and the cheap shots, Merleau-Ponty did the work decently, tastefully and unflinchingly: it was his job. He cannot claim to have uncovered the reality of the second half of the 1940s (who can?), but he took advantage of illusory French unity to stay as close as possible to the Communists, to begin necessary—and yet impossible—negotiations with them, and to lay the foundations, beyond Marx, of what he sometimes called 'a Left-wing thought.' In a sense, he failed: left-wing thought is Marxism, no more and no less. But history salvages everything except death: if Marxism is becoming *the whole of left-wing thought* today, we owe this, in the first place, to the efforts of a handful of people of whom he was one; the petty bourgeoisie, as I have said, were veering to the Left; efforts to stop their slide came from all directions, but it came to a halt on some advanced positions: to the shared desire for democratic union and reforms Merleau gave the most radical expression.

Two years of calm and then the outbreak of the cold war. Behind Marshall's homilies, Merleau was immediately able to see, and denounce, the generosity of an ogre. It was the time when groups were forming. The Communist Party hardened its line, our right fled off towards the centre; at the same point, we were beginning to hear the sound of the RPF rousing its support. The bourgeoisie raised its head again, dubbed itself 'the third force' and developed the policy of the *cordon sanitaire*. We were being pressed to take sides and Merleau refused. He had at times to cling tightly to the tiller: the Prague Coup, revolving strikes, the end of the tripartite government, the Gaullist landslide at the municipal elections. He had written, 'The class struggle is masked'; it unmasked itself. We persisted stubbornly with our offers of mediation, which no one took seriously, all the more confident that we were, in our two persons, achieving the unity of the Left because it had at the time no other representative. The RDR[19] was born, a mediating neutralism between the blocs, between the advanced fraction of the reformist petty-bourgeoisie and the revolutionary workers. I was asked to join and, allowing myself to be persuaded it shared our objectives, I accepted. Merleau, receiving requests from elsewhere, joined nevertheless so as not to disown me. It did not take me long to see I had been wrong. To live in the closest proximity to the Communist Party, to have it accept certain criticisms, we had, first, to be politically ineffectual and they had to sense that we were effectual in other ways. Merleau-Ponty was just that, standing alone with neither supporters or champions, his thought, ever new and ever recommenced, relying entirely on its own merits. By contrast,

19 RDR: Le Rassemblement Démocratique Révolutionnaire. [Trans.]

the Rassemblement, small as it was and small as it con-
sented to be, put its faith in force of numbers. As a result,
despite its immediate desire to suspend hostilities, it
immediately triggered them: where would it recruit its
revolutionary sup-porters from, if not from Communist
or related circles? The Party, up in arms, treated it from
the first as an enemy, to the astonishment of the Rassemblement's members. It was the ambiguity of this situation
that gave rise to our internal divisions: some, in disgust,
allowed themselves to drift to the Right—in general,
these were the 'organizers'. The others—the majority—
sought to remain unshakeable and to align themselves
with the social action of the PCF.[20] This latter group,
which included us, criticized the others for abandoning
the initial programme: 'Where's your neutralism?' we
asked and they immediately retorted, 'Where's yours?'

Did Merleau discover our mistake before I did? Did
he learn that political thinking cannot easily be embodied unless it is pushed to its own logical extreme and
taken up somewhere by those who have need of it? Was
it not rather that, in 1948 as in 1941, he couldn't help
feeling a little scorn for groups that were too young, that
had no roots and traditions? The fact is that he never
came to the Steering Committee, even though he was a
founder member: this, at least, is what I've been told as
I did not often go either. He may justifiably have feared

---

20 PCF: Parti communiste français—the French Communist Party.
[Trans.]

that we were distorting his project and that *Les Temps modernes* might come to be seen as the monthly organ of the RDR: he said nothing of this to me, either because he shared my incautiousness or because he did not want to reproach me with it, counting on events to remove the scales from my eyes. In short, he carried on editing the review as usual and let me carry on battling, alone and intermittently, under the banner of neutrality. In the spring of 1949, however, we were agreed that the RDR was not viable. The Mouvement de la Paix, led at the time by Yves Farge, was to hold a congress in Paris.[21] As soon as we became aware of this, the suggestion came up within the Rassemblement that we should invite a number of American personalities and, a few days after the congress, devote some 'Study Days' to peace. Clearly, we could count on the right-wing press to spread the news; in short, these pacifist 'days' were merely a political machination, backed, if not indeed inspired, by the Americans. Having been invited a little too insistently by the US Embassy to take part, a worried Richard Wright came to see me: where were we heading? Merleau joined us: we decided that the three of us would not appear at these events and we wrote a letter in all our names to explain why we were staying away; the war between the two peaces was waged without us; at the

---

21 Yves Farge (1899–1953): one of the founders in February 1948 of 'Les Combattants de la Liberté', the forerunner of the French Mouvement de la Paix, of which he was President until his death in a car accident near Tbilisi (Georgia, USSR). [Trans.]

Vél d'Hiver, an American was to be heard vaunting the merits of the atom bomb but we were not present. The activists were outraged; in June 1949, they went to the leadership to tell them what they thought of them and I took their side. We killed off the RDR and I left for Mexico, disappointed but at peace with myself. Merleau had not appeared at the congress but there could be no doubting his opinion: I realized I needed this unpleasant experience to appropriate his thought in its entirety. In fact, the so reasonable unreason of politics had been within an inch of tipping us into an anti-Communism which we execrated and to which we would, nonetheless, have had to sign up.

I saw him again in autumn: I told him I had understood his position. There would be no more active politics: the review and the review alone. I put some plans to him: why not devote an issue to the USSR? We were, it seemed, in entire agreement on this: we were becoming interchangeable. I was, then, all the more astonished that so little came of my proposals. It would have been all right if he had shown me they were absurd: but he simply let them drop, silently and glumly. The fact was that we were getting wind of the Soviet camps. Documents were sent to us at the same time as Rousset received them, but from another source. Merleau's editorial appeared in the January 1950 issue; it was to be republished in *Signs*; this time I went so far as to ask him to show it to me even before he had offered. I attended closely to every word and approved the whole piece, not least the author's consistency with his previous positions. He laid out the facts and ended the first paragraph in the following terms:

> If there are ten million concentration camp inmates—while at the other end of the Soviet hierarchy salaries and standard of living are fifteen to twenty times higher than those of free workers—then quantity changes into quality. The whole system swerves and changes meaning; and in spite of nationalization of the means of production, and even though private exploitation of man by man and unemployment are impossible in the USSR, we wonder what reasons we still have to speak of socialism in relation to it.[22]

How could the Soviet workers tolerate this disgraceful return of slavery on their soil? It was because it had come about gradually 'without deliberate intention, from crisis to crisis and expedient to expedient'.[23] Soviet citizens know the [Corrective Labour] Code, they know there are camps: what they are not perhaps aware of is the extent of the repression; if they discover it, it will be too late: they have become habituated to it in small doses.

> A good number of young Soviet heroes . . . [and] many civil servants who were favourably

---

22 Merleau-Ponty, *Signs*, p. 265.
23 Merleau-Ponty, *Signs*, p. 266.

endowed . . . who never knew discussion and the critical spirit in the sense of 1917, continue to think the prisoners are hotheads, asocial persons, men of bad will . . . And communists throughout the world expect that, by a sort of magical emanation, so many canals, factories and riches shall one day produce whole men, even if in order to produce them it is necessary to reduce ten million Russians to slavery.[24]

The existence of the camps, he said, made it possible to gauge how deluded the Communists were today. But he immediately added:

It is . . . this illusion which forbids confusing communism and fascism. If our Communists accept the camps and oppression, it is because they expect the classless society to emerge from them . . . No Nazi was ever burdened with ideas such as the recognition of man by man, internationalism, classless society. It is true that these ideas find only an unfaithful bearer in today's communism . . . The fact remains that they are still part of it.[25]

He added even more explicitly:

We have . . . the same values as a Communist . . . We may think he compromises them by

---

24 Merleau-Ponty, *Signs*, pp. 267–8.
25 Merleau-Ponty, *Signs*, p. 268.

embodying them in today's communism. The fact remains that they are ours, and that on the contrary we have nothing in common with a good number of communism's adversaries . . . [T]he USSR is on the whole situated . . . on the side of those who are struggling against the forms of exploitation known to us . . . [W]e do not draw the conclusion that indulgence must be shown towards communism, but one can in no case make a pact with its adversaries. The only sound criticism is thus the one which bears on exploitation and oppression, inside and outside the USSR.[26]

Nothing could be clearer: whatever its crimes, the USSR had this formidable advantage over the bourgeois democracies: the revolutionary aim. An Englishman said of the camps, 'They are their colonies.' To which Merleau replies, 'Our colonies are, then, *mutatis mutandis*, our labour camps.' But those camps have no other aim than to enrich the privileged classes; the Russians' camps are perhaps even more criminal since they betray the revolution; the fact remains that they were built in the belief of serving it. It may be that Marxism has been bastardized, that domestic difficulties and external pressure have distorted the regime, warped its institutions and deflected socialism from its course: still Russia cannot be compared with other nations; it is permissible to

26 Merleau-Ponty, *Signs*, pp. 268–9 (translation modified).

judge it only if one accepts its project and in the name of that project.

In short, five years after his first article, in a moment of extreme seriousness, he was going back to the principles of his politics: alongside the Party, cheek by jowl with it, never inside it. We oriented ourselves by the Party alone and outside opposition was our only attitude to it. To attack the USSR alone was to absolve the West. This uncompromising position echoes Trotskyist thinking: if the USSR is attacked, said Trotsky, we have to defend the foundations of socialism. As for the Stalinist bureaucracy, it is not for capitalism to deal with that; the Russian proletariat will see to it.

But Merleau's voice grew sombre: he spoke coldly and even his anger lacked passion and was virtually lifeless. It was as though he were feeling the first symptoms of that weariness of soul that is our general malaise. Look again at the 1945 articles and compare them and you will be able to gauge his disappointments, the attrition of his hopes. In 1945, he wrote, 'We pursue the policy of the Communist Party with no illusions.' In 1950: 'we have the same values as a communist.' And, as if the better to demonstrate the weakness of this purely moral bond: 'A Communist, it will be said, has no values . . . He has values *in spite of himself.*'[27] To be in agreement with the Communists was to attribute our maxims to them while knowing they rejected them; as for a political

27 Merleau-Ponty, *Signs*, p. 268.

understanding, there was no longer the slightest prospect of it. In 1945, Merleau forbade himself any thought or action that could possibly hinder the rebirth of the proletariat. In 1950, he simply refused to attack oppression in Russia alone: it should either be denounced everywhere or nowhere. The fact was that the USSR of 1945 seemed 'ambiguous' to him. There were 'both signs of progress and symptoms of regression'.[28] It was a nation emerging from a terrible ordeal and hope was permissible. In 1950, after the revelation of the concentration-camp system: '[W]e wonder what reasons we still have to speak of socialism in relation to it.'[29] One single concession: the USSR was, all in all, on the right side of the fence, with the forces fighting exploitation. No more than that: the revolutionary objective of 'produc[ing] whole men' was reduced in the 1950 context to being merely an illusion of the Communist parties. We might say that Merleau was, around this time, at the parting of the ways, but he was still reluctant to choose. Was he going to continue favouring the USSR in order to remain true to himself and the disadvantaged classes? Was he going to lose interest in this society based on concentration camps? If it were proved that it was made of the same clay, why would one expect any more from it than from the predatory powers? One last scruple held him back: 'The decadence of Russian communism does

28 Merleau-Ponty, *Signs*, p. 265.

29 Merleau-Ponty, *Signs*, p. 265.

not make the class struggle a myth . . . or Marxist criticism in general null and void.'[30]

Were we so sure we could reject the Stalinist regime without condemning Marxism? I received an indignant letter from Bloch-Michel. In substance, he wrote: 'How is it that you cannot understand that the Soviet economy needs a servile labour force and that each year it systematically recruits millions of underfed, overexploited workers?' If he were right, Marx had pitched us from one barbarism into another. I showed the letter to Merleau who was not convinced by it. We thought there was a legitimate passion in it, reasons of the heart but no actual Reason. No matter: perhaps if it had been better thought-out, backed by proven facts and by argument, who knows whether it would not have won us round? The difficulties of industrialization in a period of socialist accumulation, encirclement, the resistance of the peasantry, the need to secure food supplies, demographic problems, distrust, terror and police dictatorship—this whole set of facts and consequences were quite enough to overwhelm us. But what would we have said or done if it had been demonstrated that the concentrationary regime were required by the infrastructure? We would have needed to have a better knowledge of the USSR and its production regime: I went there some years later and was delivered from these fears at the point when the camps were being opened. During the winter of 1950,

---

30 Merleau-Ponty, *Signs*, p. 269 (translation modified).

we were still grimly uncertain: the Communists' strong point was that we couldn't worry about them without worrying about ourselves; however inadmissible their politics might be, we could not distance ourselves from them—at least in our old capitalist countries—without resolving on some sort of betrayal. To ask, 'How far can they go?' was the same as asking, 'How far can I follow them?' There is a morality of politics—a difficult subject that has never been clearly examined—and when politics has to betray its morality, choosing morality means betraying politics. Just try to sort all that out—especially when politics has set the coming of humanity's rule as its objective. At the point when Europe was discovering the Soviet camps, Merleau was at last catching the class struggle without its mask; strikes and repression, the massacres in Madagascar, the war in Vietnam, McCarthyism and the Red Scare in America, the Nazi revival and the Church in power everywhere, mealy mouthed, protecting renascent fascism beneath its cloak: how could we not smell the stench of the decaying carcase of bourgeois rule? And how could we publicly condemn slavery in Eastern Europe without abandoning the exploited here at home to their exploiters? But could we agree to work with the Party if it meant putting France in chains and covering it with barbed wire? What were we to do? To kick out unheedingly to Right and Left at two giants who would not even register our blows? This was the least bad solution: Merleau suggested it, for want of anything better. I could see no other way, though I was worried: we had not moved an inch, but our 'yes' had simply changed to a 'no'. In 1945, we said, 'Gentlemen, we are everyone's friends and, first and foremost, friends of our dear Communist Party.' Five years later, we were saying, 'We are everyone's enemies and the Party's only privilege is that it is still entitled to the full measure of our severity.' Without even talking about it, we both sensed that this 'soaring' objectivity would not take us far. When everyone was being forced to choose, we had not chosen; and we had perhaps been right. At present, our universal peevishness could perhaps put off the choice for a few months more. But we knew that, had we been editors of a daily or a weekly, we should long ago have had to take the plunge or go to the wall. The relatively small-circulation character of the review gave us some respite, but our—initially political—position was in danger of turning gradually into moralism. We never descended to the level of the 'beautiful soul', but fine sentiments flourished in our vicinity while manuscripts became scarcer: we were losing momentum, people no longer wanted to write for us.

In China, they showed me the statues of two traitors in a ditch; people have been spitting on them for a thousand years and they are all shiny, eroded by human saliva. We were not yet shiny, Merleau and I, but the process of erosion had begun. We were not being forgiven for rejecting Manichaeism. On the Right, butchers' boys had been recruited to insult us: they were given *carte blanche*; they showed their behinds to the critics and the critics doffed their hats to them, proclaiming them the 'new generation'. Ultimately, all the fairies had watched over their cradles but one, the 'talent fairy', and they disappeared for lack of it: they needed just a hint of it, no more, but it had been denied them at birth. They would be starving to death today if the Algerian War were not feeding them: crime pays. They made a lot of noise, but did little harm. On the other flank, things were more serious: our friends in the Communist Party had not come to terms with the article on the camps. We had left ourselves open to attack and we really got it from them. It didn't bother me. I was called a rat, a hyena, a viper and a polecat, but I liked this bestiary; it took me out of myself. Merleau was more upset by it: he still remembered the comradely relations of 1945. There were two phases: at first, he was insulted in the morning in the public prints, then late in the evening his Communist friends made their highly secretive excuses. This went on until a day came when, in order to simplify matters, these same friends combined the two jobs, writing the articles at dawn and apologizing for them at dusk. Merleau suffered less from being insulted by intimates than from no longer being able to respect them. I would say today that they were possessed by a literally insane violence that was the product of a war of attrition being fought elsewhere, the effects of which were felt in our provincial backwater: they were trying to see themselves as other than they were and couldn't quite manage it. Merleau saw their faults, I think, and not their problem, this provincialism. This is understandable, since he knew them in everyday life. In short, he moved away from them because they wanted him to: the Communist Party had tolerated these fringes of critical sympathy on its periphery, but it had not liked them. From 1949 onwards, it decided to eliminate them: the friends outside the Party were requested to shut their mouths. If any of them publicly expressed reservations, they sickened him until he turned into an enemy. In this way the Party proved to its activists—and each activist thought he proved to himself—that free examination of the dogma was the beginning of betrayal. It was *themselves* that Merleau's friends loathed in him. How much anguish there was in all this and how it all came out after the seismic shock of the Twentieth Congress! Merleau knew the score: the Communists' bad tempers did not reduce him to anti-Communism. He took the blows but gave none back: his attitude was simply to do right and let others say what they wanted. In short, he carried on with the project. No matter: they denied him oxygen; they exiled him once again into the thin atmosphere of solitary life.

The Communist Party, born of a historical upheaval, a party that had its traditions and its constraints, had appeared to him in the past, even from afar, as offering a possible community: now he lost it. He had many friends who were not Communists, of course, and who remained true to him: but what did he find in them or for them, but the affectionate indifference of the pre-war period? They met together around a table and ate together, so as to pretend for a moment they had a common task: but these very varied human beings, still shattered by history's intrusion into their private lives, shared nothing but a scotch or a leg of lamb. This amounted, of course, to recognizing that something had died: he realized at last that the Resistance had crumbled; but these perceptions have no deep truth to them unless we feel them to be our own death gaining ground on us. I saw Merleau often in the winter and spring; he showed little sign of nerves, but was extremely sensitive: without entirely understanding him, I felt he was dying a little. Five years later, he would write: 'The writer well knows that there is no possible comparison between the rumination on his life and the clearer, more precise things it may have produced (in his work).' This is true: everyone ruminates; one broods on the insults one has suffered, the disgust one has felt, the accusations, recriminations and pleadings—and then one tries to piece together fragmented experiences that have neither rhyme nor reason to them. Like each of us, Merleau knew those wearisome repetitions from which a sudden enlightenment sometimes springs. That year, there was neither light nor a bolt from the blue. He tried to take the measure of things, to put himself back at that crossroads where his own story intersected with the history of France and the world, where the course of his thinking emerged from the course of events: this is what he had tried to do, and succeeded in doing, as I have said, between 1939 and

1945. But in 1950 it was both too late and too early. 'I'd like to write a novel about myself,' he told me one day. 'Why not an autobiography?' I asked. 'There are too many questions without answers. In a novel I could give them imaginary solutions.' We must not let this recourse to the imagination mislead us: I would remind the reader of the role phenomenology allots to it in the complex movement that ends in the intuiting of an essence. And yet, even so, his life defied explanation; in meditating upon it, patches of shade emerged, breaks in continuity. Didn't the fact that he had pitched himself, against his will, into this open conflict with his former friends mean that he had made a mistake at the outset? Or was he not bound to take upon himself—at the risk of becoming torn by it—the shifts and turns of an immense move-ment that had produced him, the mainsprings of which lay beyond his control. Or, alternatively—as he had sug-gested in 1945 as a mere conjecture—had we not fallen, for a period at least, into non-meaning? Perhaps there was nothing left for us to do but *endure* by holding on to a few rare values? He kept his post at *Les Temps modernes* and chose not to change any of his activities. But 'rumi-nating on his life', taking him back towards his origins, slowly took him away from day-to-day politics. This was his good fortune; when people leave the marginal zone of the Communist Party, they have to go somewhere: they usually walk for a time and end up on the Right; Merleau never committed this betrayal: rejected, he took refuge in the depths of his inner life.

Summer came. The Koreans began fighting each other. We were separated when the news reached us: each of us commented off our own bat, as we saw fit. We met up at Saint-Raphaël, in August, for a day: too late. We were happy to see each other's gestures again, hear each other's voices, to meet up again with all those familiar oddities for which friends the world over love their friends. There was only one flaw: our ideas, already formed, were incommunicable. From morning to night we talked only of the war, first sitting still by the water, then over dinner, then on the terrace of a cafe surrounded by scantily clad holidaymakers. We debated as we walked and then again at the station as I waited for my train. But to no avail; we were deaf to each other. I spoke more than he did, I fear, and not without vehemence. He replied gently and curtly: the sinuous thinness and child-like mischievousness of his smile made me hope he was still hesitating. But no: he never trumpeted his decisions; I had to accept he had made up his mind. He repeated gently, 'All that remains is for us to keep silent.'

'Who is us?' I said, pretending not to understand.

'Well, we at *Les Temps modernes*.

'You want us to shut up shop?'

'No, but I want us to say no more about politics.'

'Why?'

'They're fighting.'

'Yes, they are, in Korea.'

'Tomorrow they'll be fighting everywhere.'

'But even if they were fighting here, why would we keep quiet?'

'Because . . . It's brute force that will decide. Why speak, since brute force has no ears?'

I got on the train. Leaning out of the window, I waved, as one does, and I saw he was waving back, but I sat dumbfounded till I reached my destination.

I charged him, very unjustly, with wanting to gag criticism at the point when the guns were beginning to rumble. This was far from his mind; he had merely come up against an overwhelming fact: the USSR, he thought, had attempted to compensate for its inferiority in weaponry by acquiring a strategic position. The first thing this meant was that Stalin thought war inevitable: it was no longer a question of averting war, but of winning it. But war had only to appear inescapable to one of the blocs for it to become so. It would have been all right if the capitalist world had attacked first: the world would have been blown up, but humanity's venture would have retained a meaning, even when shattered. Something would be dead, but it would at least have made an effort to be born. But since the preventive aggression was coming from the socialist countries, history would merely have been the winding-sheet of our species. The game was up. For Merleau-Ponty, as for many others, 1950 was the crucial year: he thought he saw the Stalinist doctrine without its mask and he judged it to be a Bonapartism. Either the USSR was not the homeland of socialism—in which case, socialism existed nowhere and was, no doubt, unviable—or else socialism was indeed this—this abominable monster, this police state, this predatory power. In short, Bloch-Michel had been unable to convince Merleau that socialist society rested on serfdom; but Merleau convinced himself that it had engendered—whether by chance, necessity or both together—an imperialism. This did not, of course, mean that he had opted for the other monster, capitalist imperialism. 'But what can you say?' he said. 'They are as bad as each other.' This was the great change: he had no desire to rail against the Soviet Union—'Why should I? People are exploited, massacred and plundered the world over. Let's not take it all out on the one party.' It merely lost all privilege in his eyes; it was a predatory power like all the others. He believed at this point that the internal workings of history had perverted its course once and for all; it would carry on in a state of paralysis, deflected by its own *dejecta*, till it finally came to grief. All meaningful discourse could only, therefore, be lies: all that remained was to withhold one's complicity, to remain silent. He had wanted at first to retain what he felt to be valid in the two systems; he wanted to make a gift to the better one of what the other had achieved. In his disappointment, he had subsequently resolved to denounce exploitation wherever it occurred. After further disappointment, he calmly decided not to denounce anything anywhere ever again, till such point as a bomb, from either East or West, put an end to our brief histories. Being first affirmative, then negative, then silent, he had not shifted an inch. This moderation would be difficult to understand, however, if one did not see it as the calm exterior of a man committing suicide: I have already said that his worst acts of violence were depth charges that harmed only himself. Even in the most wildly raging anger, some hope remains: in this calm, funereal refusal, there was none.

I didn't think these things through as he did; that is what preserved me from melancholy. Merleau made light of the Koreans, but I could see nothing else. He moved too quickly to global strategy and I was mesmerized by the blood: the fault, as I saw it, was with the horse traders at Yalta who had cut the country in two. We were both wrong, out of ignorance, but not without some excuse: where at the time would we have acquired our knowledge? Who would have revealed to us that a military canker was gnawing at the USA and that civilians, in Truman's day, already had their backs to the wall? How in August 1950 would we have guessed MacArthur's plan and his intention to take advantage of a conflict to give China back to the Chinese lobby? Did we know of Syngman Rhee, the feudal prince of a state reduced to poverty, and of the designs of the agricultural South on northern industry? The Communist press barely spoke of any of this: they knew little more about it than we did and merely denounced the crime of the imperialist forces, i.e. the Americans, without taking the analysis any further. And, then, they compromised their credibility with a preliminary lie: the only fact that had been established was that the northern troops had been the first to cross the 38th Parallel; now, the Communist press stubbornly maintained the opposite. We know the truth today, which is that the US army, in league with Seoul's feudal overlords, drew the Communists into a trap: there were frontier incidents daily and they took advantage of them; the South made such obvious troop movements that the North, deceived, committed the enormous error of striking first to forestall an attack that was never intended. It is a failing of mass parties that they think they can connect with popular thinking—the only deep, true thought—by offering it truths adjusted to its taste. I no longer have any doubt, for example, that in this wretched business the warmongers were the feudal South and the US imperialists. But I have no doubt either that the North attacked first. The Communist Party's task was not easy: when it acknowledged the facts, if only to bring out their meaning, its enemies everywhere presented it as 'confessing' to them. If it denied the facts, its friends discovered the lie and backed away. It chose to deny them in order to remain on the offensive. But it was less than a year ago that we had discovered the existence of the Soviet camps: we were still distrustful and ready to believe the worst. In reality, the USSR deplored this conflict, which might drag it into a war that it could not easily win: yet it had to support the North Koreans for fear of losing its influence in Asia. By contrast, the young China entered the fray, knowing itself to be the object of American designs, but everything required it to do so: revolutionary fraternity, its permanent interests and its international policy. We, however, had not enough information in the summer of 1950 to see who was playing which role. Merleau believed in Stalin's guilt because he had to believe in it. I didn't believe in anything; I was floundering about, uncertain. This was my good fortune; I didn't have the same temptation to believe that the lights were going out or that it was the year 1000 and the curtain was going up on the Apocalypse: I viewed this blaze from afar and could make out nothing distinct.

In Paris, I met up again with Merleau. Colder and darker. Some of our friends, his wife told me, were devoutly hoping I would blow my brains out the day the Cossacks crossed our borders. Naturally, they were calling for Merleau's brains too. Suicide did not tempt me and I laughed; Merleau-Ponty observed me and did not. Thoughts of war and exile came to his mind. Lightly, with that puckish air I always saw him adopt when things might be turning serious: he would, he said, be a lift attendant in New York. An embarrassing joke: this was another version of suicide. If war broke out, it would not be enough just to stop writing, you would have to refuse to teach. Imprisoned in a lift cage, he would simply push buttons and mortify himself with silence. Such seriousness is not common and may surprise the reader. Yet he had it, we had it, and I do still.

On one point we were in agreement with the good people who wanted our skins: in politics, you have to pay.
We were not men of action, but wrong ideas are crimes
at par with wrong acts. How did he judge himself? He
did not say, but he seemed worried and worrying: 'If
ever,' I said to myself, 'he passes judgement on himself,
his concealed rage will push him immediately to the
point of carrying it out.' I often wondered later how his
cold anger against the USSR could have turned into a
surliness directed against himself. If we had fallen into
barbarism, then we could not say a word or even keep
silent without behaving as barbarians: why did he blame
himself for sincere, carefully thought-out articles? The
world's absurdity had simply stolen his thoughts; there
was nothing more to it. He answered this point in *Signs*
with an explanation of Nizan that also covers his own
case:

> One can understand, then, the objections Sartre
> makes today to the Nizan of 1939 and why they
> are without weight against him. Nizan, he says,
> was angry. But is that anger a matter of mood?
> It is a mode of understanding which is not too
> inappropriate when fundamental meaning-
> structures are at stake. For anyone who has
> become a Communist and has acted within the
> party day after day, things said and done have a
> weight because he has said and done them too.
> In order to take the change in line of 1939 as

he should, Nizan would have had to have been a puppet. He would have to have been broken . . . I recall having written from Lorraine, in October, 1939, some prophetic letters which divided the roles between us and the USSR in a Machiavellian fashion. But I had not spent years preaching the Soviet alliance. Like Sartre, I had no party: a good position for severely doing justice to the toughest of parties.[31]

Merleau-Ponty was never, by any stretch of the imagination, a Communist; he was not even tempted to be. There was no question of him 'acting within the Party', but he lived its daily life through friends he had chosen. He did not blame himself for things said and done, but for the comments he had penned about them, for his decision never to offer a critique before having attempted to understand and to justify. He had been right, however, and one knows something only if one gives of oneself. But the consequence was that he suffered for having given of himself for nothing. He had said, 'Historical man has only one way of suffering barbarism, and that is to make it.' He was the victim of those he had defended so patiently because he had made himself their accomplice. In a word, he abandoned politics the moment he felt he had lost his way in it. With dignity, but guiltily: he had dared to live; now, he walled himself up. He was of course to change his mind about

31 Merleau-Ponty, *Signs*, pp. 32–3.

all this later and come to other conclusions; but that was in 1955: this sorrow weighed on his heart for five years.

There was no shortage of people to explain his turn-about in class terms: he was, they said, a liberal petty-bourgeois; he went as far as he could and then stopped. How simple that is! And those who say this are petty-bourgeois raised as liberals who, nonetheless, opted for the Manichaeism he rejected. It was, in fact, history's fault that the thread was broken: she wears out the men she uses and rides them to death like horses. She chooses actors, transforms them to their very core by the role she forces on them, then, at the slightest change, dismisses them and takes on entirely new ones, whom she throws untutored into the scrimmage. Merleau began work in the milieu that had been produced by the Resistance: with the Resistance's passing, he believed the unity it had produced lived on to a degree in some sort of future humanism which the classes, by their very struggle, could construct together. He 'followed the Communist Party line', yet refused to condemn the cultural heritage of the bourgeoisie out of hand. Thanks to this effort to hold on to both ends of the chain, the circulation of ideas in France was never entirely halted: as everywhere, there was a loathing for intelligence, but until 1958 we never knew any intellectual McCarthyism. Moreover, the official thinkers of the Communist Party condemned his ideas, yet the best of them always knew those ideas had to be taken up and that it behoved Marxist anthropology to assimilate them. But for Merleau, is it conceivable that Tran Duc Tao would have written his thesis and attempted to annex Husserl to Marx?

In many archaic religions, there are sacred personages who perform the function of *binders*: everything has to be linked and attached through them. Politically, Merleau played such a role. He had come to politics in a time of union and refused to break up that union; his role was to bind. I believe the ambiguity of his heuristic Marxism—he said that it could not be sufficient, but also that we had nothing else—created a favourable climate for encounters and discussions that will continue. In this way, he made the history of this post-war period, as much as an intellectual can. Conversely, while being made by him, history also made him. Refusing to set his seal on breaches between people, hanging on with each hand to continents that were drifting apart, he returned in the end, without illusions, to his old idea of catholicity: on either side of the barricade there are only human beings; hence human inventiveness is being born everywhere: it is to be judged not on its origins, but on its content. It is enough that the 'binder' strain every sinew to keep the two terms of the contradiction together, that he hold back the explosion for as long as he is able: creative works, the product of chance and reason, will attest that the reign of the human is possible. I cannot decide whether this idea was behind its time or ahead of it in October 1950. One single thing is sure: it was not timely. The globe was cracking apart. There wasn't a single thought that didn't express some prejudice and aim to function as a weapon, not a single bond that didn't form without others breaking; to serve one's friends, everyone had to spill the blood of enemies. Let us be clear here: others, besides the 'binder', condemned Manichaeism and violence. But they did so precisely because they were Manichaean and violent: in a word, to serve the bourgeoisie. Merleau-Ponty was the only one who did not celebrate the triumph of discord, the only one not to tolerate—in the name of our 'catholic' vocation—love everywhere becoming the obverse of hatred. History had given him to us; well before his death, it took him away.

At *Les Temps modernes*, we had put politics on the back burner. It must be admitted that our readers did not notice this right away: we were, at times, so far behind that we came round to talking about things when everyone had forgotten them. However, in the long run, people grew angry: being uncertain, they called for enlightenment and it was our bounden duty either to provide them with it or to confess that we were as lost as they were. We received irritated letters; the critics weighed in too; in an old issue of *L'Observateur* I recently found a 'Review of reviews' which took us sternly to task. We were each aware of these criticisms, sometimes learning of them from each other, but we never discussed them: that would have meant reopening the debate. It rather got on my nerves: did Merleau realize he was *imposing* his silence upon us? But then I would talk myself round: the review belonged to him, he had defined its political orientation and I had followed him; if our silence were the ultimate consequence of this, I had to go on following him. His smiling sullenness was harder to bear: he seemed to be reproaching us for having accompanied him into this hell-on-earth, and sometimes for having dragged him into it. The truth is that he could sense our discord growing and it pained him.

We emerged from this impasse without having made any decisions, without speaking. Dzelepy and Stone sent us good, well-informed articles which showed up the war, as it was happening, in a new light. I found that these articles confirmed my opinions. As for Merleau, they didn't contradict his own: we didn't go back over the origins of the conflict. However, he didn't like the articles much, but he was too honest to reject them: I didn't dare insist that we take them. I can't claim that we published them: they published themselves and we found them in the review. Others followed, finding the way to the printers by themselves. This was the beginning of a surprising transformation: having lost its political director, *Les Temps modernes* stubbornly went on obeying him, despite his change of heart. That is to say, it took a radical turn of its own volition. We had long-standing collaborators, most of whom did not meet us often: they changed position to remain as close as they

could to the Communist Party, believing they were following us in this, when in fact they were dragging us
along with them. Young people came in to the review
on the basis of the reputation Merleau had made for it:
it was, they thought, the only publication which, in this
age of iron, retained both its preferences and its clear-
sightedness. None of these newcomers was a Communist, yet none wanted to veer from the Party line. In this
way they put *Les Temps modernes* back, in other—more
brutal—circumstances, in the position Merleau had
given it in 1945. But this meant overturning everything:
to keep our distance from the Communists, it was necessary in 1951 to break with all the rest of what still
called itself the Left. Merleau remained silent: more
exactly, he gagged himself with a hint of sadism. He
forced himself, out of professionalism and the demands
of friendship, to let through this stream of tendentious
articles, which addressed themselves to our readership
over his head and which, in a roundabout way—by way
of anything, even a film criticism—gave vent to a confused, muddled, impersonal opinion that was no longer
his without yet being entirely mine. In this way we both
discovered that, over these six years, the review had
acquired a kind of independence and that it directed us
as much as we directed it. In a word, during the interreg-
num years 1950–52, a skipperless vessel itself recruited
officers who kept it afloat. In those days, when Merleau
looked at this little sardine rushing along in the wake of

a whale, if he still told himself 'That is the fruit of my labours! . . .' then he must have swallowed many draughts of gall. He had fixed himself fast to the review, to which he had given life and which he kept alive day after day. I think he suddenly found himself in the position of a father who, having only yesterday treated his son as a child, suddenly finds himself face to face with a mulish, almost hostile adolescent, who has 'got into bad company'. Sometimes I tell myself that our common mistake was to remain silent *even then*, when we were still uncertain and uncommitted . . . But no, the die was cast.

The world developed a war psychosis and I developed a bad conscience. All over the West, people wondered in nonchalant tones but wild-eyed, what the Russians would do with Europe when they had occupied the whole of it. 'For they certainly will,' said the drawing-room generals. The same people spoke smugly of the Breton redoubt, that bridgehead the Americans would maintain in Finistère to facilitate future landings. Fine: if there was fighting on our soil, no problem: none of us would be spared. But other oracles thought the USA would look to other continents for the real battlefields and would abandon us, out of convenience, to the USSR. What would we do in that case? One answer was given by some young middle-class maidens: in a girls' grammar school in Paris, an entire class vowed to resort to collective suicide. The black heroism of these poor children said a great deal about the fright their parents felt. I heard some very dear friends, former Resistance fighters, coldly declare that they would take to the hills. 'This time,' I said, 'there's a danger you'll be shooting at Frenchmen.' I saw from their eyes that that would not trouble them, or rather that they had stubbornly arrived, out of hysteria, at this unreal decision. Others chose realism: they would take a plane to the New World. I was, in those years, a little less mad: for no other reason, perhaps, than a lack of imagination, I didn't believe in the Apocalypse. Yet my mood grew sombre; in the Metro a man shouted out, 'I'll be glad when the Russians get here!' I looked at him: his life-story was etched on his face; in his place, I would perhaps have said the same. I asked myself, 'What if, nonetheless, this war did take place?' People kept telling me, 'You'd have to leave. If you stay, then either you'll broadcast on Soviet radio or you'll go to a camp and we won't hear from you again.' These predictions didn't frighten me much, because I didn't believe in an invasion. Yet they made an impact on me: they were, in my eyes, mind games which, pushing things to extremes, revealed to everyone the need to choose and the consequences of their choices. Staying, they told me, meant collaboration or death. And leaving? To live in Buenos Aires with the wealthy of France, while abandoning my poor compatriots to their fate, would also be a way of collaborating: with the enemy class. But it was your class, you will say. Yet what does that mean? Is that any proof it is not still the enemy of humanity? If there must be betrayal, as Nizan said in *The Watchdogs*, let it be the smallest number doing it for the good of the largest.

These gloomy fantasies made me feel really up against it. Everyone had chosen; in my turn, I tried for a moment to linger in neutralism: several of us supported Rivet's candidacy;[32] but the Communist Party had diverted away the potential supporters to his right: he suffered a crushing defeat.

Some Communists came to see me about the Henri Martin affair.[33] They were trying to bring together intellectuals of every stamp, from the well- regarded to the smarmy and the wanton, to bring the matter before the public. As soon as I'd taken a look at the business, it seemed so stupid that I joined in unreservedly with the protestors. We decided to write a book about the affair and I left for Italy; it was spring. From the Italian newspapers I learned of Duclos' arrest, the theft of his notebooks and the carrier pigeons farce.[34] These sordid

---

32 Paul Rivet (1876-1958): one of the founders of the pre-war Comité de Vigilance des Intellectuels Antifascistes, which was one of the organizations that contributed to the emergence of the French Popular Front. [Trans.]

33 Henri Martin: a French sailor who was arrested for sabotage in March 1950 in French Indochina. Though cleared of that charge, he was sentenced to five years' imprisonment for distributing anti-war propaganda. He was freed in August 1953 after a national campaign to liberate him, in which Sartre played a prominent role. The book to which Sartre refers here, and which contained contributions from Michel Leiris, Vercors, Francis Jeanson, Jacques Prévert and Hervé Bazin among others, is L'Affaire Henri Martin (Paris: Gallimard, 1953). [Trans.]

34 The Communist leader Jacques Duclos had been arrested after a demonstration. Two dead pigeons in his car were alleged to have been 'carrier pigeons' for communicating with Moscow. [Trans.]

childish tricks turned my stomach: fouler things were done, but none that was so revealing. My last ties were broken, my view transformed: an anti-Communist is a cur; this is my firm opinion and I shall not change it. People will think me very naïve and, indeed, I had seen many other things of this kind that had not stirred me. But after ten years of ruminations, I had reached breaking point; only the merest trifle was needed. In the language of the Church, this was a conversion. Merleau too had been converted, in 1950. We were both conditioned, but in opposite ways. Our disgusts, slowly accumulated, caused us in an instant to discover, in the one case, the horror of Stalinism, in the other, the horror of his own class. On the basis of the principles it had inculcated in me, on the basis of its humanism and its 'humanities', on the basis of liberty, equality and fraternity, I swore a hatred of the bourgeoisie that will end only when I do. When I hastily returned to Paris, I had to write or suffocate. I wrote, day and night, the first part of 'The Communists and Peace'.[35]

Merleau could not be suspected of any indulgence for the police methods of a dying regime: he seemed

---

35 Jean-Paul Sartre, 'Les Communistes et la paix', Part 1, *Les Temps modernes*, 81 (July 1952); Part 2, *Les Temps modernes*, 84–85 (October–November 1952); Part 3, *Les Temps modernes* (April 1954). Reproduced in Jean-Paul Sartre, *Situations VI* (Paris: Gallimard, 1964), pp. 80–384; *The Communists and Peace*, with *A Reply to Claude Lefort* (Martha H. Fletcher and Philip R. Berk trans.) (New York: Braziller, 1968). [Trans.]

surprised by my eagerness, but he strongly encouraged me to publish this essay, which was supposed to be merely article-length. When he read it, he needed only a glance: 'The USSR wants peace,' I said, 'it needs it, the only threat of war comes from the West.' I said not a word about the Korean War, but, despite that precaution, it seemed I had premeditatedly taken a systematically opposite line to our political director, that I had contradicted his views point by point. I had in fact written at breakneck speed, with rage in my heart, joyously and tactlessly. When the best prepared conversions explode, one finds the joy of the storm: all around is blackest night, except where the lightning is striking. Not for a moment did I think to spare his feelings. For his part, he chose rather to be amused by my hotheadedness and was not angry. A while later, however, he pointed out that some of our readers were not with me on this: of course they shared my opinion on the way our government had acted, but in their view I was being too soft on the Communists. 'What do you tell them?' I asked. It so happened that printed below this first study were the words: 'To be continued.' 'I tell them,' he said, 'Next instalment in the next issue.' Around 1948, the non-Communist Left had, in fact, drawn up an essay plan that acquired classic status: (1) Thesis: rehearsal of the vileness of the government and its crimes against the working classes; the Communist Party was pronounced right; (2) Anti-thesis: the unworthiness of the Political Bureau was highlighted, together with the mistakes it had made; (3) Conclusion: both were as bad as each other and a middle course was pointed out, with unfailing mention here of the Scandinavian countries. As Merleau saw it, I had developed only the thesis; he was still hoping— though without too many illusions—that the antithesis would follow.

It did not. Nor was the continuation printed in the next issue. I was, in reality, out of breath. And I realized I knew nothing. Just railing against a Prefect of Police doesn't bring insight into one's times. I had read everything, but everything had to be read again. I had only one guiding thread, but it was enough: the inexhaustible, difficult experience of the class struggle. I did the re-reading. I had some intellectual muscle and I set about using it, not without tiring myself. I met Farge. I joined the Peace Movement. I went to Vienna. One day I took my second article to the printers, though it was, in fact, merely an outline. I had entirely set aside the 'Third Force'-style essay plan: far from attacking the Communists, I declared myself a fellow traveller. At the end, once again, I wrote, 'To be continued', but there could no longer be any doubt. Merleau didn't see the article until the second proofs. Adding to my guilt, I didn't show them to him myself: he read them at the point when we had to make up the issue. Why hadn't I shown him my manuscript when he always showed me his without fail? Had I decided, once and for all, to take myself seriously?

I don't believe so. And I don't believe either that I wanted to escape his admonishments or objections. I would blame, rather, that heedlessness of rage that aims straight for the goal and brooks no precautions. I believed; I knew; I had cast off my illusions: as a result, I would not climb down over anything. In our virtually private publication, you had to shout to be heard: I would shout; I would place myself alongside the Communists and would proclaim this to all and sundry. I shall not give the objective reasons for my attitude: they are of no importance here; I shall simply say that they alone counted, that I regarded them as urgent, and that I still do. As for the emotional reasons, I can see two: I was propelled along by the new team; they wanted us to take the leap; I could count on their approval. And then I now see that I bore a bit of a grudge against Merleau for having imposed his silence on me in 1950. The review had been drifting for two years and I couldn't bear it. Let each one judge: I have no excuse, I don't want any. What may be of interest in this adventure—which we both found painful—is that it shows in what ways discord may arise in the heart of the most loyal friendship and the closest agreement. New circumstances and an outdated institution—there were no other reasons for our conflict. The institution was our silent contract. Valid when Merleau spoke and I said nothing, this agreement had never clearly defined our respective domains. Each of us, without speaking of it even to himself, had appropriated the review. There was on the one hand, as in *The Caucasian Chalk Circle*, an official, nominal paternity, mine—and in everything connected with politics it was only that[36]—and, on the other, an adoptive paternity, five years of jealous care. Everything came to a head suddenly and exasperatedly. We realized that each of us, by his silences as much as by his words, was compromising the other. We needed to have only one set of ideas; and this was the case so long as I did not think for myself. But once there were two heads under the same hat, how were we to choose the right one? Looking at the matter from outside, it will seem that events themselves decided: this is true, but it is rather a facile explanation. It is true, in general, that empires crumble and parties collapse when they are not swimming with the tide of history. Even so, we must admit that this idea, which is perhaps the most difficult of all, is handled incautiously by most writers. But how can we use what may be applied— though not without care—to the great social forces, to explain, the growth, life and death of micro-organisms like *Les Temps modernes*? The overall movement was not without its small-scale catastrophes. And, then, however it might be, we had to live the venture ourselves, to accept the sentence passed on us, to carry it out and, as he said later, institute it. With wrong on each side and, in each of us a futile goodwill.

Merleau could have broken things off; he could have provoked a quarrel or written something against me. He abstained, eloquently, from all these things. For a time

---

36 In the other fields I would say not that the situation was reversed but that we worked together.

we remained this strange couple: two friends who still liked each other, each of whom was stubbornly opposed to the other and who had between them only one voice. I admire his moderation all the more for the fact that there were, at the time, several loudly trumpeted defections from the review: one of our longest-standing collaborators left us in a great hurry for the *Nouvelle Nouvelle Revue Française*, where he began by rounding on the 'Hitlero-Stalinists' and by speaking in glowing terms of Lucien Rebatet.[37] I wonder what there is left of him now: perhaps a rather too self-conscious smattering of *ennui*, somewhere in the provinces, and nothing more.

The years that followed brought several entertaining crack-ups of the same kind. To fill these gaps and drum up articles, I assembled our collaborators at my flat every other Sunday. Merleau-Ponty attended assiduously, being always the last to arrive and the first to leave, conversing in hushed tones with anyone and everyone on all subjects except *Les Temps modernes*. Yet he had allies in the camp: Claude Lefort, who disapproved of my position, Lefèvre-Pontalis,[38] who wasn't interested in politics, Colette Audry, who feared my excesses, and Erval.[39]

---

37 Lucien Rebatet (1903–72): a fascist, anti-semitic writer who had been a prominent journalist on the magazine Je suis partout before and during the Nazi Occupation. [Trans.]

38 Jean-Bertrand Pontalis, better known today as a Lacanian psychoanalyst and man of letters. [Trans.]

39 The pseudonym of François Emmanuel (1914–99), the Romanian-born journalist, critic and publisher. [Trans.]

It would not have been hard for Merleau to assume the leadership of a strong opposition: he refused to do so on principle—a review isn't a parliamentary assembly—and from friendship. He forbade himself to influence the group while noting, without liking the fact, that the group was influencing me. The majority was, as it happened, lining up before his eyes behind the critical fellow-traveller position he had just abandoned; given the virulence of anti-Communism, the majority was even contemplating toning down the critical aspect and stressing the 'fellow-travelling'. Above all, I think Merleau found these meetings laughable and their product worthless. In the long run they became so and his silence had its part in bringing this about. But what would he have said? I never failed to ask his opinions; he never ventured them. It was as though he was letting me know it was no good asking me about details when I hadn't deigned to consulted him on the main issue. He probably took the view that I was salving my conscience cheaply and didn't want to help me in that. In fact, my conscience was clear and I felt Merleau was wrong to refuse to participate. This grievance will seem misplaced; when all is said and done, I was asking him to work on a venture he had openly disavowed. I recognize this: but, after all, he remained one of our number and then, from time to time, he couldn't stop himself taking some initiative—usually a felicitous one. Though he had abandoned his role of political director after 1950, he still remained editor. In these ambiguous situations, which one maintains in being to avoid a break, everything both parties do turns bad.

But there were more serious reasons for our misunderstanding and they were of a different order. I saw myself as remaining faithful to his thinking of 1945, while he was abandoning it. He saw himself as remaining faithful to himself and felt that I was betraying him. I claimed that I was carrying on his work and he accused me of wrecking it. This conflict came not from either of us but from the world. And we were both right. His political thinking came out of the Resistance; in other words, it emerged from the united Left. Within that unity, it could slide towards the most extreme radicalism, but he needed this triple-entente environment: the Communist Party guaranteed the practical efficacy of common action; the allied parties assured him that that action would retain its humanism and certain traditional values, while lending them real content. When, around 1950, everything broke apart, he saw only wreckage; in his eyes, it was my folly to cling to one bit of flotsam, expecting that the pieces of wreckage would rebuild the lost vessel on their own. For my part, I made my decision when the Left was smashed to pieces; my opinion was that it had to be reconstituted, though not at the top, but from the bottom up. We had, of course, no contact with the masses and hence no power. But our task remained clear: in the face of the unholy alliance between the bourgeoisie and the socialist leaders, there was no other course than to snuggle up to the Party and call on the others to join us. We had to attack the bourgeoisie unrelentingly, expose its policies and defuse its feeble arguments. We would not, of course, recoil from criticizing the Communist Party and the USSR. But we recognized that changing them was out of the question—an impossible task. We wanted to foreshadow future agreements for our readers by setting before them this tiny example of an accord with the Communists that had in no way detracted from our freedom of judgement. I was able, in this way, honestly to take the view that I was espousing Merleau-Ponty's attitude.

In fact, the contradiction was not in *us*, but, from 1945 onwards, in our position. To be for the whole was to refuse to choose between its parts. The privilege Merleau accorded the Communists wasn't a choice in their favour: merely a preferential regime. When the moment to choose came, he remained faithful to himself and scuppered his own efforts, so as not to survive the shipwrecked unity. I, however, as a newcomer, chose the Party precisely in the name of unity: that unity could not be rebuilt, I thought, unless it were done around the Party. In this way, at a few years' remove, the same idea of union had led the one of us to reject a choice it had forced upon the other. Structures and events together determined everything; France is so constituted that the Party will not take power there on its own: we have therefore to think, first, in terms of alliances. Merleau could still see the tripartite government as a legacy of the Popular Front. But in 1952, without the demographic structure of the country having changed, I could no longer see the Third Force—a mere mask for the Right— as coterminous with the unity of the masses. Yet, power could not be taken from the Right without gathering together all the forces of the Left: the Popular Front remained the necessary means to triumph at the point when the cold war rendered it impossible. While waiting for an alliance to come about that seemed only a distant possibility, we had to maintain that possibility day after day by forming local alliances with the Party. Not choosing on the one hand, choosing on the other— but for the five years' difference, the two attitudes were pursuing the same objective. Two attitudes? There was, rather, just the one, which set us against each other as adversaries, by compelling each of us to stress one of its two contradictory components. In order to remain true to what he wouldn't accept, Merleau forgot his desire for union. And, to give future unity its chance, I forgot my universalism and chose to begin by increasing the disunion. These words will seem abstract; in fact we had to live through these historical determinations: that is to say, we put our whole life into them, our passions, our skins. I mocked his 'spontaneity': in 1945, union seemed to be achieved, he could just let himself be carried along. He mocked my naivety and voluntarism; in 1952, there was no union any longer; was wishing for it in the abstract enough to bring it about? The truth is that we each found the job to suit our talents: Merleau when it was time for subtleties, myself when the time of the hired killers had arrived.

Lefort and I had some lively discussions and I suggested that he criticize me in the review itself. He accepted and submitted a rather nasty article. I got angry and wrote a reply in the same tone. As a friend to both of us, Merleau found himself, against his wishes, with a new task: he had to play the role of mediator. Lefort had had the courtesy to submit his article to Merleau and I did the same with mine. My article exasperated him: with his customary sweetness, he informed me that he would leave once and for all if I didn't remove a certain paragraph, which was, as it seems to me, needlessly violent. I seem to remember that Lefort made some sacrifices too. All the same, our two texts had a spiteful tone to them. Merleau was fond of both of us and felt every one of the blows we dealt each other. Without being entirely in agreement with Lefort, he felt closer to him than to me: this freed his tongue. And mine. We launched into a long and futile argument that cascaded from one subject to another, one conversation to another. Is there such a thing as the spontaneity of the masses? Can groups derive their cohesion from themselves? Ambiguous questions which sent us off at times to politics, to the role of the Communist Party, to Rosa Luxemburg and Lenin, and at times to sociology, to existence itself or, in other words, to philosophy, to our 'styles of life', to our 'anchorage-points', to ourselves.

With every word we bounced from a consideration of world affairs to the development of our own moods and back again. Beneath our intellectual divergences of 1941, which we had accepted so serenely when we were just arguing over Husserl, we discovered to our stupefaction, conflicts that had their source in our childhoods—and even in the elementary rhythms of our organisms. We went on to uncover the surreptitious presence in one of us of a slyness, a smugness and a mania for activism, that covered over his disorientation and, in the other, retractile sentiments and a determined quietism. Naturally, nothing in this was entirely true or entirely false: our ideas became confused because we were putting the same ardour into convincing, understanding and accusing each other. This passionate dialogue, carried on at a halfway point between good and bad faith, began in my office, continued in Saint-Tropez and was recommenced in Paris at the Café Procope and later at my flat. I travelled. He wrote me a very long letter. I replied, on a day when it was 40 degrees in the shade, which didn't improve matters. What were we hoping for? Ultimately, for nothing. We were doing our 'break-up work' in the sense in which Freud has so well demonstrated that mourning is 'work'. I believe this sullen two-handed rumination, this endless repetition that led us nowhere, was going to end in gradually exhausting our patience, in breaking the bonds between us one by one by little angry bursts, in casting shadows on the transparent nature of our friendship to the point of making us strangers to each other. If this undertaking had reached its end, we would have quarrelled. Fortunately, an incident intervened that interrupted it.

A Marxist I had bumped into by chance offered to write for us on 'the contradictions of capitalism'. This was, he said, a familiar subject, but little understood, and he would shed new light on it. He was not a member of the Party but a party unto himself and one of the most rigid; he had such a sense that he was doing me a favour that he talked me round. I forewarned Merleau, who knew the man but said nothing. I had to be out of Paris and the article was submitted in my absence. It was worthless. As editor-in-chief, Merleau-Ponty could not be persuaded to allow it to appear without adding an introductory paragraph, which was, all in all, an apology to our readers. He took the opportunity to criticize the author in two lines for not having even mentioned the contradictions of socialism: this would be for another day, no doubt? On my return, he told me nothing of all this; one of our collaborators put me in the picture and I got myself a set of proofs and read the article beneath its introductory paragraph. The less defensible the article seemed to me, the more irritated I was by that paragraph. Having put the issue 'to bed', as they say, Merleau was in his turn away from the office and I wasn't able to get hold of him. Alone and in a state of merry rage, I took out the introductory paragraph and the article appeared without it. You can guess the rest. A few days later, Merleau received the final proofs of the review, noticed his text had been cut and took it extremely badly. He grabbed the telephone and informed me of his resignation—for good this time. We spoke for more than two hours. Sitting in an armchair by the window, a very gloomy Jean Cau heard half the conversation and thought he was witnessing the last moments of the magazine.[40] We accused each other of abusing our power; I offered him an immediate meeting and tried in every way possible to make him reverse his decision: he was immovable. I didn't see him again for a few months; he didn't come to *Les Temps modernes* and never had anything else to do with it.

If I have told this idiotic story, I have done so, first and foremost, for its pointlessness. When I think back to it, I feel both that it was heartbreaking and that it 'had to end like that'. Like that: badly, stupidly, inevitably. The stage was set, the end decided in advance. As in *Commedia dell'Arte*, it only remained for us to improvise the break-up; we handled it badly, but, for good or ill, we acted out the scene and moved on to the next ones. I don't know which of us was the more guilty and it's not a question that excites me much: in fact, the ultimate guilt was a preordained part of our two roles; we had

---

40 Prolific writer Jean Cau (1925–93) was Sartre's secretary at this time. He won the Prix Goncourt in 1961 for his novel *La pitié de Dieu*. In later years, he switched political camps dramatically and became involved with GRECE and the so-called New Right. [Trans.]

established, long before, that we would part with wrong on both sides and on some puerile pretext. Since we could no longer continue to work together, we had to part or have the review disappear.

Without *Les Temps modernes*, the events of 1950 would have had little impact on our friendship: we would have discussed politics more often or taken more care not to speak of it. Ordinarily politics affects people obliquely and they are unaware of anything except a muffled tremor or an indecipherable anxiety. Unless, that is, it seizes them by the throat and knocks them flying: even in that case, they will not realize what has happened to them. But chance has only to put the tiniest means of influencing or expressing the movement of history into their hands and the forces that shape our lives are immediately laid bare and show us the shadow we cast on the dazzling wall of objectivity. The review was nothing: it was just a sign of the times like a hundred others. But no matter: it belonged to history and through it the two of us experienced our standing as historical objects. It was our objectivization; through it the course of events provided us with our charter and our twofold role: we were at first more united than we would have been without it, then more divided. This is only natural: once caught in the mechanism, we are completely dragged into it; the little freedom that remains to us lies entirely in the moment when we decide whether to get involved or not. To put it succinctly, beginnings are our affair; thereafter we have to will our destinies.

The beginning was not a bad one. It was so for a single reason that is still a mystery to me: against the desire of all our collaborators, and against my desire, Merleau had claimed the weakest position from day one. The position of doing everything and not being named, of refusing to have a status to defend him against my moods or attacks: it was as though he had wanted to derive his power only from a living agreement, as though his fragility would be his most effective weapon, as though his moral authority would alone have to underwrite his functions. He had no sort of protection: for that reason, he was not bound by anything or anyone. He was present among us and as much in charge as I was. And he could be light and free as air. If he had agreed to his name going on the cover, he would have had to fight me and perhaps even overthrow me: but he had envisaged this possibility from the first day and declined on principle a battle that would have needlessly demeaned us both. When the fateful day came, a telephone call sufficed. He had made his decision, he informed me of it and disappeared. Yet there were sacrifices: for him, for me and for *Les Temps modernes*. We were all victims of this cleansing murder: Merleau cut off a part of himself, leaving me to grapple with fearful allies who, he thought, would grind me down or reject me as they had rejected him; he abandoned *his* review to my incompetence. This aggressive expiation must have absorbed the greater part of his resentment: in any event it allowed us to interrupt our break-up 'work' and rescue our friendship.

To begin with, he avoided me. Did he think the sight of me would revive his grievances? Perhaps. It seems to me, however, that he wanted to keep open the prospect of some kind of shared future. I would meet him at times; we stopped a moment to talk together; when we were about to part, I would suggest we meet up again the next day or the next week. He replied politely and firmly, 'I'll call you,' but he did not. Yet, another 'work' had begun: the stilling of grievances and a *rapprochement*. This was halted by grief: in 1953 Merleau lost his mother.

She meant as much to him as his own life; more exactly, she *was* his life. He owed his infant happiness to the attentions she had lavished on him; she was the clear-sighted witness of his childhood: thanks to that, when exile came, she remained its guardian. Without her, the past would have been swallowed by the sands; through her, it was preserved, out of reach but intensely felt; until the time came to mourn his mother, Merleau-Ponty experienced that golden age as a paradise that retreated a little more each day and as the fleshly, daily presence of the woman who had bestowed it on him. All the con-nivances of mother and son carried them back to ancient memories; thus, as long as she lived, Merleau's banish-ment retained a degree of sweetness and could be reduced at times to the bare difference that separates two inseparable lives. As long as there were two of them reconstructing and, at times, reviving the long prehistory of his actions, his passions and his tastes, he still had hope of regaining that immediate concord with everything that is the good fortune of children who have been loved. But when his mother died, the wind slammed all the doors shut and he knew they would never open again. Memories *à deux* are rites: the survivor is left only with dried leaves, with words. Meeting Simone de Beauvoir a little after this, Merleau-Ponty told her, quite casually and with that sad cheerfulness with which he masked his sincere remarks, 'I am more than half dead.' Dead to his childhood—for the second time. He had dreamed of achieving salvation: in his youth through the Christian community, as an adult through his political companionships. Twice disappointed, he suddenly discovered the reason for these defeats: to 'save' oneself on all levels, 'in all orders', would be to recommence one's earliest years. We repeat ourselves endlessly, but we never begin again. Seeing his childhood go under, he understood himself: he had never wished for anything but to return to it and that impossible desire was his particular vocation, his destiny. What was left of it? Nothing. He had already been silent for some time: silence not being enough any longer, he turned into a recluse, leaving his office only to go to the Collège de France. I did not see him again until 1956 and his best friends now saw him less.

I have, however, to indicate what was happening in him during the three years that separated us. But, as I have forewarned my readers, my object is merely to recount the adventure of a friendship. I am, for this reason, interested in the history of his ideas rather than in the ideas themselves, which others will be able to describe in detail, and better than I would. It is the man I want to restore, not as he was for himself but as he lived in my life, as I experienced him in his. I do not know how truthful I shall be. I shall seem questionable and it will seem I am depicting myself negatively by the way I paint him: this I admit. I am, at any rate, sincere: I am describing what I took to be the case.

Pain is emptiness: others might have remained simulacra of hermits, hollow men. But, at the same time as it cut him off from us, his pain led Merleau back to his initial meditation, to the good fortune that had made him so unfortunate. I am struck by the unity of Merleau's life. Since the pre-war years, this young Oedipus who had revisited his origins had wished to understand the rational unreason that produced him. Just as he was getting close to it and writing the *Phenomenology of Perception*, history jumped at our throats. He wrestled with it without interrupting his quest. Let us call this the first period of his thinking. The second began in the last years of the Occupation and continued until 1950. His thesis completed, he seemed to abandon that investigation and turn to the questioning of history and the politics of our time. But his concern had changed only in appearance: everything connects up, since history is a form of envelopment and we are 'anchored' in it, since we have to situate ourselves historically not in an *a priori* fashion, by some 'soaring' thought, but through the concrete experience of the movement that carries us along: if we read him closely, Merleau's commentaries on politics are merely a political experience becoming, by itself and in all senses of the term, a *subject* of meditation; if writings are acts, let us say that he acts in order to appropriate his action and to find himself, at a deep level, in that action. From the general perspective of history, Merleau is an intellectual from the middle classes, radicalized by the Resistance and blown off course by the fragmentation of the Left.[41] Seen for himself, his was a life that turned round on itself to grasp the emergence of the human in its singularity. Cruel as it was, it is clear that his disappointment of 1950 was to be of use to him: it removed him from our sad arenas, but, in so doing, it offered him an arena that was neither quite the same nor entirely different—that enigma that is the self. Not that he sought, like Stendhal, to understand the individual that he was but, rather, in the manner of Montaigne, he wanted to comprehend the person, that matchless mix of the particular and the universal. Yet that was not enough: there remained knots to untie; he was tackling these when the

---

41 Clearly, we could all be defined in this same way, except that the degrees of drift are variable and sometimes run in the opposite direction.

death of his mother supervened and cut through them. It is admirable that, in his sadness, he made this ill-fortune his own, elevating it to the status of strictest necessity. Though it had been foreshadowed for some years, the third period of his meditation began in 1953.

In the beginning, it was both a renewed investigation and a wake. Thrown back on himself for a third time by death, he tried to use it to cast light on his birth. To the newborn, this visible-seer who appears in the world of vision, something must *happen*: something, anything, even if it is only dying. This initial tension between appearance and disappearance he term 'primordial historicity': it is in and through this that everything occurs; it hurls us, from the very first moment, into an inflexible irreversibility. To survive birth, if only for a moment, is an adventure; and it is an adventure also not to survive it: one cannot escape this unreason he terms our contingency. It is not enough to say that we are born to die: we are born to death.

At the same time, being alive, he prevented his mother from disappearing entirely. He no longer believed in an afterlife; if, however, in his last years, he happened to reject being numbered among the atheists, this was not out of consideration for his one-time burst of Christianity, but to leave a chance for the dead. Yet this precaution was not enough: in reviving a dead woman through the worship of her, what was he doing? Was he reviving her in fantasy or *instituting* her?

Life and death; existence and being: to carry out his two-pronged investigation, he tried to pitch his tent at this crossroads. In a sense, none of the ideas he advanced in his thesis changed; in another, nothing was recognizable any longer: he plunged into the dark night of non-knowledge, in search of what he now called the 'fundamental'. In *Signs*, for example, we read: 'What interests the philosopher in anthropology is just that it takes man as he is, in his actual situation of life and understanding. The philosopher it interests is not the one who wants to explain or construct the world, but the one who seeks to deepen our insertion in being.'[42]

At the level of presence and absence, the philosopher appears, blind and all-seeing: though *knowledge* claims to explain or construct, he does not even want to *know*. He lives in this mix of oxygen and thin gases called the True, but he doesn't deign to itemize the truths—not even to distribute them to our schools or textbooks. He does nothing but deepen himself: he allows himself to slide, while still alive, without interrupting his undertakings, into the sole, derisory abyss accessible to him; to seek within himself the door that opens on to the night of what is not yet self. This is to define philosophy as a meditation in the Cartesian sense of the word—that is to say, as an indefinitely sustained tension between existence and Being. This slim, ambiguous dividing

---

42 Merleau-Ponty, 'From Mauss to Claude Lévi-Strauss', in *Signs*, p. 123.

line is the origin: to think, one must *be*; the tiniest thought exceeds being, instituting it for others; this happens in a trice: it is birth, absurd and definitive, that indestructible *e*vent that changes into *ad*vent and defines the singularity of a life by its calling to death: it is the work [*oeuvre*], opaque and wild, retaining being in its folds; it is the undertaking, an unreason that will endure in the community as its future *raison d'être*; it is, above all, language, this 'fundamental', for the Word is merely the Being cast into the heart of man to extenuate itself in a *meaning*; in short, it is man, emerging at a stroke, moving beyond his presence to Being and towards his presence to others, moving beyond his past and towards his future, moving beyond everything and himself towards the sign: for this reason, Merleau tended, towards the end of his life, to grant ever greater scope to the unconscious. He doubtless agreed with Lacan's formula, 'The unconscious is structured like a language.' But, as a philosopher, he had placed himself at the opposite pole to psychoanalysis: the unconscious fascinated him both as a fettered speech and as the hinge of Being and existence.

One day, Merleau-Ponty took against dialectics and abused it. Not that he didn't accept the division on which it is based; he explains in *Signs* that the positive always has its negative and vice versa; they will, as a consequence, pass eternally one into the other. These things go round, so to speak, and the philosopher will go round with them. It is for him to follow the circuits of his object scrupulously and in a spirit of discovery; he must spiral down into the darkness. Merleau-Ponty acquired the habit of pursuing every 'No' until he saw it turn into a 'Yes' and every 'Yes' until it changed into a 'No'. He became so proficient, in his latter years, at this game of 'hide the slipper' that he positively made a method of it. I shall term this inversion. He jumped from one standpoint to another, denied and affirmed, changed more into less and less into more: all things are contraries and all are also true. I shall give just one example of this: 'At least as much as he explains adult behaviour by a fate inherited from childhood, Freud shows a *premature* adult life in childhood, and . . . for example, a first choice of his relationships of generosity or avarice to others.'[43] *At least as much*: in his writings contradictory truths never fight against each other; there is no risk of shackling the movement, of causing a break-up. And are they indeed, strictly speaking, contradictory? If this were even admitted, it would have to be acknowledged that contradiction, weakened by this giratory impulse, loses its role as 'engine of history' and represents in his eyes the sign of paradox, the living mark of fundamental ambiguity. In short, Merleau is quite happy with thesis and antithesis; it is the synthesis he rejects: he reproaches it with turning the dialectic into a construction set. By contrast, his revolving structures leave no room for a conclusion; each

---

43 Merleau-Ponty, 'Man and Adversity', in *Signs*, p. 229.

in its way illustrates the merry-go-round of Being and existence. As children of clay, we should reduce ourselves to imprints on the earth if we did not begin by denying it. Let us invert, then: we, whose most immediate existence is the negation of what is, what do we do from our first moment to our last but announce Being, institute it, restore it by and for others, in the milieu of intersubjectivity? Institute it, announce it—all well and good. As for seeing it face to face, that we must not expect: we know only its signs. Thus the philosopher will never stop running round in circles, nor will the roundabout stop turning:

> This being—which is glimpsed through time's stirrings and always intended by our ... perception and our carnal being, but to which there can be no question of our being transported because to abolish its distance would be to take away its consistency of being—this being 'of distances', as Heidegger will put it, which is always offered to our transcendence, is the dialectical idea of being as defined in the *Parmenides*— beyond the empirical multiplicity of existent things and as a matter of principle intended through them, because separated from them, it would be only lightning flash or darkness.[44]

44 Merleau-Ponty, *Signs*, p. 156. It was a question at that point of characterizing the present moment of philosophical research. Merleau lent it these two features: 'existence and dialectics'. However, a few months before, he had given a lecture at the Rencontres

Merleau still has his flirtatious moments: he still speaks in this text of dialectics. Yet it isn't to Hegel he refers but to Parmenides and Plato. The appropriate method with meditation is to draw an outer line around one's subject and revisit the same places time and again. What is it, then, that meditation can make out? An absence? A presence? Both? Refracted by a prism, the outer being scatters, becomes multiple and inaccessible; but, as part of the same movement, it is also internalized, becomes the inner being—entirely and constantly present, yet not losing its intangibility. And, naturally, the opposite is also true: the inner being within us, our innermost recess, fiercely guarded and grave, constantly manifests its oneness with Nature, that indefinite deployment of outer being. Thus, circling and meditating, Merleau remains faithful to his spontaneous thinking, a slow rumination shot through with bolts of lightning: it is this which he sets up discreetly as a method, in the form of a decapitated dialectic.

In the end, it was this descent into Hell that enabled him to find the profoundest merry-go-round of all. It was a discovery of the heart, as is proved by its striking, sombre density. I shall tell how he informed me of it almost two years ago: the man paints himself, subtle and

---

Internationales de Genève on the thought of our time. Remarkably, he did not say one word about Dialectics: rather, in referring to our problems, he avoided the word contradiction and wrote: 'Embodiment and the question of the other are the labyrinth of thinking and sensibility among our contemporaries.'

laconic as he was, in these remarks, tackling problems head on when he seems merely to be brushing at them from the side. I asked him if he was working. He hesitated: 'I'm perhaps going to write on Nature.' To whet my appetite, he added: 'I read a sentence in Whitehead that made an impression on me: "Nature is in tatters".' As the reader will already have guessed, not another word was added. I left him without having understood: at that time I was studying 'dialectical materialism' and for me the word 'Nature' evoked the full extent of our physical and chemical knowledge. Another misunderstanding: I had forgotten that Nature for him was the tangible world, that 'decidedly universal' world in which we encounter things and animals, our own bodies and others. I did not understand him until his last article, 'Eye and Mind', was published.[45] That long essay was, I imagine, supposed to form part of the book he was writing: at any rate, he constantly refers and alludes there to an idea that was going to be expressed, but remains unformulated.

More hostile than ever to intellectualism, Merleau enquires into painters and their manual, untutored thinking: he tries to grasp the meaning of painting from the works themselves. On this occasion, Nature reveals its 'threads and tatters' to him. How, he says more or less, does that mountain in the distance announce itself to

---

45 Maurice Merleau-Ponty, 'Eye and Mind', in James Edie (ed.), *The Primacy of Perception* (Carleton Dallery trans.) (Evanston: Northwestern University Press, 1964) [Maurice Merleau-Ponty, *L'Œil et l'esprit* (Paris: Gallimard, 1961)—Trans.]

us? By discontinuous and, at times, intermittent signals, sparse, insubstantial phantasms, shimmerings, shadow-play; this dusty thing strikes us by its sheer insubstantiality. But our eye is, precisely a 'computer of Being';[46] these airy signs will settle into the heaviest of terrestrial masses. The gaze no longer contents itself with 'glimps[ing] . . . being . . . through time's stirrings': it would seem now that its mission is to form its—ever-absent—unity out of multiplicity. 'And so that unity does not exist?' we shall ask. It does and it does not, just like the defunct coat whose presence haunts the threads and tatters like Mallarmé's rose that is 'absent from all bouquets'. Being *is* through us, who *are* through it. All this, of course, requires the Other; this is how Merleau understands Husserl's 'difficult' assertion that 'transcendental consciousness is intersubjectivity.' No one, he thinks, can see, unless he is at the same time visible: how would we grasp what *is* if we *were not*? We are not speaking here of a mere '*noesis*', producing its noematic correlative through appearances. Once again, in order to think, one must first *be*. The thing, constituted by each of us out of all things—always a unity, but an indefinitely chamfered unity—consigns each of us, through the others, to our ontological status. We are the sea; as soon as it emerges each piece of driftwood is as uncountable as the waves, through them and like them absolute.

---

46 Merleau-Ponty speaks of the eyes as *computeurs du monde*, 'computers of the world'. See 'Eye and Mind', *The Primacy of Perception*, p. 165. [Trans.]

The painter is the privileged artisan, the best witness of this mediated reciprocity. 'The body is caught in the fabric of the world, but the world is made of the stuff of my body.' A new spiralling, but deeper than the others since it relates to the 'labyrinth of embodiment'. Through my flesh, Nature is made flesh; but, conversely, if painting is possible, then the lineaments of being that the painter perceives in the thing and fixes on the canvas must designate, in the very depths of himself, the 'flexions' of his being. 'Only on condition of being self-figuring does the painting relate . . . to anything whatever among empirical things; it is a spectacle of things only by being the spectacle of nothing . . . showing how things make themselves things and the world a world.' It is just this that gives 'the painter's occupation an urgency that exceeds all others'. By representing outer being, he presents others with inner being, *his* flesh, their flesh. But 'present' is too weak a word here: culture, says Merleau, is a 'coming-into-being'. So the artist has this sacred function of instituting being amid men; this means going beyond the 'layers of raw being of which the activist is unaware' towards that eminent being that is *meaning*. The artist has this function, but each of us has it also. 'Expression,' he says, 'is the *fundamental* quality of the body.' And what is there to express except Being: we do not make a single movement without restoring being, instituting it and rendering it present. Primordial historicity, our being born unto death, is the surging from the deep through which the event becomes man and, by naming things, recites his being. This is also the history of groups in its most radical aspect: 'What but history are we to call this [milieu] in which a form burdened with contingency suddenly opens up a cycle of futurity and commands it with the authority of that which is established?'

These are, in their beginnings, his last thoughts: of his last philosophy, 'burdened with contingency', gnawing patiently at chance and interrupted by that chance, I have said that I saw it begin with a discovery of the heart. Against mourning and absence, it was he in his turn who was discovering himself: he was the true 'computer of Being'. He had a handful of memories and relics left, but our gaze reveals the being of the mountain with fewer resources than that: from the tatters of memory, the heart will wrest the being of the dead; out of the *e*vent that killed them it will make their *ad*vent; it is not simply a question of restoring their eternity to the lost smile and the words: to live will be to deepen them, to transform them into themselves a little more each day, by our words and our smiles, without end. There is a progress of the dead and it is our history. In this way, Merleau made himself his mother's guardian, as she had been the guardian of his childhood; born through her unto death, he wanted death to be a rebirth for her. For this reason, he found more real powers in absence than in presence. 'Eye and Mind' contains a curious quotation: Marivaux, reflecting in *Marianne* on the strength and dignity of the passions, praises men who take their own lives rather than deny their being.[47] What Merleau liked about these few lines is that they uncovered an indestructible slab of stone beneath the transparency of the shallow stream that is life. But let us not be tempted to think he is returning here to Cartesian substance: hardly has he closed the quotation marks and taken up his pen on his own account than the slab shatters into discontinuous flickerings, becomes that ragged being that it is our lot to be, which is perhaps merely a disordered imperative, and which a suicide will sometimes put back together better than a living victory. By a movement of the same kind, since this is our rule, we shall institute the being of the dead in the human community by our own being, and our being by that of the dead.

How far did he go, then, in these dark years that changed him into himself? At times, reading him, one would say that Being invents man in order to be *manifested* by him. Did it not happen from time to time that Merleau, inverting the terms and standing things on their head, thought he glimpsed in us, 'ungraspable in immanence', some sort of transcendent mandate? In one of his articles, he congratulates a mystic on having written that God is below us. He adds, more or less, 'Why not?' He dreams of an Almighty who would need human beings, who would be in question in everyone's heart and

47 *La Vie de Marianne*, begun in 1727, is an unfinished novel by Pierre de Marivaux. The novel was written in sections, eleven of which appeared between 1731 and 1745. [Trans.]

would remain the total Being, the one that intersubjectivity is re-instituting infinitely, the only one we would
push to the limit of its being and which would share
with all of us the insecurity of the human adventure.
This is clearly just a metaphorical indication. But the
fact that he chose it cannot be seen as insignificant. It
has everything in it: both stroke of inspiration and risk;
if *L'Être*[48] is below us, a gigantic ragged pauper, it will
take only an imperceptible change for it to become *our
task*. God, the task of man? Merleau never wrote that,
and he forbade himself to think it: there is nothing to
say that he did not sometimes dream of it, but his
researches were too rigorous for him to put forward anything he had not established. He worked unhurriedly;
he was waiting.

It has been claimed that he had moved closer to Heidegger. There is little doubt of this, but we must be clear
what we mean. So long as his childhood was safeguarded
for him, Merleau had no need to radicalize his quest.
With his mother dead, and his childhood swept away
with her, absence and presence, Being and Non-Being
flowed into each other. Merleau, through phenomenology and without ever leaving it, wanted to connect with
the imperatives of ontology; that which is no longer, is
not yet, never will be: it was for man to give Being to
beings. These tasks emerged out of his life, out of his
mourning; he found in them the opportunity to reread

---

48 'Being' or 'the Being'. [Trans.]

Heidegger, to understand him better, but not to give in to his influence: their paths crossed and that was all. Being is the sole concern of the German philosopher; despite what is at times a shared vocabulary, man remains the main concern of Merleau. When the former speaks of 'openness to being', I smell alienation. Admittedly, we should not deny that the latter has sometimes penned some troubling words. These, for example: 'The irrelative henceforth is not nature in itself or the system of the apprehensions of the absolute consciousness, nor indeed is it man, but that "teleology" that must be written and thought between quotation marks—the framework and articulation of the being that is accomplished through man.' The quotation marks don't make any difference. All the same, it was said only in passing. It is regrettable that a man can write today that the absolute is not man; but what he denies to the human realm, he does not grant to any other. His 'irrelative' is, in fact, a relation of reciprocity that is closed upon itself: man is designated by his basic calling, which is to institute Being, but Being is similarly designated by its destiny, which is to accomplish itself through man. I have told how, twice at least— in the Christian community and in the fraternity of political combat— Merleau had sought to envelop himself in immanence and had run up against the transcendent. While more than ever avoiding recourse to the Hegelian synthesis, his last thinking attempts to resolve the contradiction he experienced in his life: the transcendent will be poured into immanence; it will be dissolved in it, while being protected, by its very intangibility, from annihilation; it is now merely absence and supplication, merely infinite weakness dragging its omnipotence along. Is this not, in a sense, the fundamental contradiction of all humanism? And can dialectical materialism—in the name of which many will want to criticize this meditation—do without an ontology? Looking closer, indeed, and if we set aside the absurd theory of reflection, would we not find in it, discreetly announced, the idea of a layer of raw being producing and underpinning action and thought?

No, the man who a few months before his death wrote, 'When the lightning flash that is man blazes out, everything is given in that very instant,' never ceased to be a humanist. And then what? To accomplish Being is indeed to consecrate it: but that means to humanize it. Merleau does not claim that we should lose ourselves so that Being may be but, quite the contrary, that we shall institute Being by the very act that causes us to be born to the human [*naître à l'humain*]. More Pascalian than ever, he reminds us once again: Man is absolutely distinct from the animal species, but precisely in the respect that he has no original equipment and is the place of contingency, which sometimes takes the form of a kind of miracle . . . and sometimes the form of an unintentional adversity.[49]

This is sufficient to say that man is never either the animal of a species or the object of a universal concept

---

49 Merleau-Ponty, 'Man and Adversity', in *Signs*, p. 240.

but, from the moment he emerges, the splendour of an event. But he draws the same lesson from the humanist Montaigne: Montaigne 'rejects in advance the explanations of man a physics or metaphysics can give us, because it is still man who "proves" philosophies and sciences, and because they are explained by him rather than he by them . . .'[50] Man will never think man: he *makes* him at every moment. Is not this the true humanism: man will never be a total object of knowledge; he is the subject of history.

In the last works of the sombre philosopher, it is not difficult to find a certain optimism: nothing comes to anything, but nothing is lost. An endeavour is born, institutes *its* man at a stroke—the whole of the man in a lightning flash—and perishes with him or survives him extravagantly to end, in any event, in disaster; yet, at the very moment of calamity, it opens a door to the future. Spartacus struggling and dying is the whole of man: who can say better than this? A word is the whole of language gathered into a few sounds; a picture is the whole of painting. 'In this sense,' he says, 'there both is progress and there is not.' History is constantly establishing itself in our prehistoric milieu; with each lightning flash, the whole is illuminated, instituted, frays at the edges and, deathless, disappears. Apelles of Cos, Rembrandt and Klee each in their turn *presented Being to the gaze* in a particular civilization and with the means available to them. And long before the first of them was born, the

---

50 Merleau-Ponty, 'Reading Montaigne', in *Signs*, p. 202.

whole of painting was already made manifest in the caves of Lascaux.

Precisely because he is constantly summing himself up in this ever-recommenced lightning-flash, there will be a future for man. Contingency of Good, contingency of Evil: Merleau no longer either favoured or condemned anyone. Adversity had brought us within an inch of barbarism; miracles, always and everywhere possible, would bring us out of it. Since, 'spontaneously, every gesture of our body and language, every act of political life . . . takes others into consideration and surpasses itself, in its singularity, in the direction of the universal,' then even though it is in no sense necessary or promised, and even though we call on it not so much to improve us in our being as to clean up the detritus of our lives, a *relative* progress has to be the most probable conjecture: 'Experience will, very probably, end up eliminating the false solutions.' It is in this hope, I believe, that he agreed to write a number of political commentaries for *L'Express*. The Soviet and Western blocs were two growth economies, two industrial societies, each riven by contradictions. Above and beyond the different regimes, he would have liked to have identified common demands at the infrastructural level or lines of convergence at least: it was a way of remaining faithful to his own thinking. Once again, the point was to reject the Manichaean option. There had been unity; after the loss of that minor paradise, he had wanted to denounce exploitation everywhere, then he had walled himself up in silence: he came back out to seek after reasons for hope everywhere. Without any illusions—'*la virtú*' and nothing more. We are twisted creatures: the ties binding us to others are distorted; there is no regime that could, in itself, rectify that distortion, but perhaps the men who will come after us—all men together—will have the strength and the patience to undertake this task.

The course of our thinking separated us a little more each day. His mourning and voluntary reclusiveness made a *rapprochement* more difficult. In 1955, we almost lost each other completely, by abstraction. He wrote a book on the Dialectic in which he attacked me fiercely.[51] Simone de Beauvoir replied no less fiercely in *Les Temps modernes*: it was the first and last time we argued in print. By publishing our differences, it seemed we would inevitably render them irremediable. Quite the contrary: at the point when friendship seemed dead, it began to blossom again imperceptibly. We had no doubt been too careful to avoid violence: it needed a little to eliminate the last few grievances and for him to get everything off his chest once and for all. In short, the quarrel was short-lived and we met up again not long afterwards.

It was in Venice in the early months of 1956, where the European Society of Culture had organized discussions between East and West European writers. I was

---

51 Maurice Merleau-Ponty, *Les aventures de la dialectique* (Paris: Gallimard, 1955); *Adventures of the Dialectic* (Joseph Bien trans.) (Evanston: Northwestern University Press, 1973). [Trans.]

there. As I sat down, I noticed that the seat alongside mine was empty. I leaned over and saw Merleau-Ponty's name on the card: we had been put together because they thought it would be to our liking. The discussion began, but I was only half listening; I was waiting for Merleau—not without trepidation. He came. Late as usual. Someone was speaking. He slipped behind me on tiptoe and touched me lightly on the shoulder; when I turned round, he smiled. The conversations went on for several days: we were not entirely in agreement, except that we both became irritated listening to an over- eloquent Italian and an excessively naive Englishman who had been deputed to scuttle the project. But among so many people of such diversity, some older than us, others younger, we felt united by a self-same culture and experience, meaningful only to us. We spent several evenings together, a little uneasily and never alone. It was all right. Our friends who were present protected us from ourselves, from the temptation of prematurely re-establishing our intimacy. As a consequence, we merely talked to one another. Though neither of us had any illusions about the significance of the Venice discussions, we both wanted them to take place again the next year—he because he was a 'binder', I to 'privilege' the Left: when it came to drafting the final communiqué, we found ourselves of the same mind. It was nothing, and yet it was proof that a shared task could bring us together.

We met again—in Paris, in Rome and again in Paris. Alone: this was the second stage. The unease was still there, but was tending to disappear; another feeling emerged, one of tender affection: such disconsolate, mildly funereal affection brings together exhausted friends, to whom strife has left nothing in common but their quarrel and whose quarrel has one day ended for want of anything to argue over. That thing had been the review: it had united, then separated us; it no longer even separated us. Our cautiousness in our relations with each other had almost led us to fall out: aware of this now, we were careful never to spare each other's feelings. But too late. Whatever we did, each of us now failed to engage the other. When we explained our positions, it seemed to me rather as though we were exchanging news of our respective families—auntie Mary is having an operation, nephew Charles has got his 'A levels'—and we were sitting side by side on a bench with blankets over our knees, tracing out signs in the dust with the ends of our walking sticks. What was missing? Neither affection, nor esteem, but a shared undertaking. Our past activity had been buried without it having being able to separate us, but it took its revenge by making 'retired' old friends of us.

We had to wait for the third stage without forcing things. I waited, certain that our friendship would be recovered. We were united in condemning the war in Algeria unreservedly; he had sent his *légion d'honneur* back to the Guy Mollet government and we were both opposed to the fledgling dictatorship that was Gaullism. We were not perhaps agreed on how to fight it, but that would come: when Fascism is on the rise, it reunites lost friends. I saw him in the March of that same year. I was giving a lecture at the École normale and he came along. I was touched by this. For years it had been I who was always angling for meetings, proposing rendezvous. For the first time, he spontaneously went out of his way. Not to hear me rehearse ideas that he knew by heart, but to see me. At the end of the lecture, we met up together with Hyppolite and Canguilhem. For me, it was a happy moment. Later, however, I learned that he had apparently felt a persistence of the unease between us. This was not remotely the case, but unfortunately I had the flu and was rather groggy. When we parted, he had uttered no word of his disappointment but for a moment I sensed a stiffening. I took no notice of it: 'Everything is as it was,' I told myself, 'it will all begin again.' A few days later, I learned of his death and our friendship ended on this last misunderstanding. Had he lived, it would have been dissipated as soon as I returned. Perhaps. With his death, we shall remain for each other what we always were: unknowns.

Without a doubt, Merleau's readers can know him; he has 'made an appointment with them in his work'; every time I become his reader, I shall know him and know myself better. A hundred and fifty pages of his future book have been saved from the wreckage[52] and

---

52 This is presumably a reference to *Le visible et l'invisible, suivi de notes de travail*, published posthumously, together with Merleau's notes for its continuation, by his friend Claude Lefort (Paris: Gallimard, 1964). See Maurice Merleau-Ponty, *The Visible and the*

then there is 'Eye and Mind', which says everything, provided one knows how to decipher it: we shall, all of us together, 'institute' this thinking we find in tatters; it will be one of the prisms of our 'intersubjectivity'. At a moment when Mr Papon, the Prefect of Police, sums up the general view when he states that nothing surprises him any longer, Merleau provides the antidote by being surprised by everything. He is a child scandalized by our footling grown-up certainties, a child who asks the scandalous questions the adults never answer: why do we live? Why do we die? Nothing seems natural to him— either the fact that there is a history or that there is a nature. He doesn't understand how it can be that every necessity turns into contingency and every contingency ends up in necessity. He says this and we, reading him, are dragged into this whirligig, from which we shall never extract ourselves. Yet it is not us he is questioning: he is too afraid we shall hit up against reassuring dogmatisms. This questioning will be something between himself and himself, because 'the writer has chosen insecurity'. Insecurity: our basic situation and, at one and the same time, the difficult attitude that reveals this situation to us. It is not appropriate for us to ask for answers from him; what he teaches us is how to deepen an initial enquiry; he reminds us, as Plato did, that the philosopher is the person who experiences wonderment, but, more rigorous in this than his Greek master, he adds

---

Invisible, Followed by Working Notes (Alphonso Lingis trans.) (Evanston, IL: Northwestern University Press, 1968). [Trans.]

that the philosophical attitude disappears the minute that wonderment ceases. Conversely, to those who predict that philosophy will one day take over the world, he replies that if man were one day happy, free and transparent to other men, we ought to be as amazed by that suspect happiness as we are at our present misfortunes. I would happily say, if the word did not seem suspect to him through overuse, that he had managed to rediscover the internal dialectic of questioner and questioned, and that he had pushed it as far as the fundamental question we avoid with all our alleged responses. To follow him, we have to give up two contradictory securities between which we constantly waver, for we reassure ourselves ordinarily by the use of two concepts that are opposite in nature but equally universal. Both of these take us as objects, the first telling each of us that he is a man among men and the second that he is an Other among others. But the former is worthless because man is constantly making himself and can never think of himself in his entirety. And the latter deceives us, because we are in fact similar, insofar as each of us differs from all. Jumping from the one idea to the other, the way monkeys jump from one branch to another, we avoid singularity, which is not so much a fact as a perpetual postulation. Severing our links with our contemporaries, the bourgeoisie confines us within the cocoon of private life and cuts us up with its scissors into *individuals*—that is to say, molecules without history that drag themselves from one moment to the next. Through Merleau we find ourselves singular again, through the contingency of our anchorage in nature and in history or, in other words, through the temporal adventure that we represent within the human adventure. Thus history makes *us* universal to precisely the same degree that we make *it* particular. This is the considerable gift Merleau bestows on us by his relentless determination to keep on digging in the same spot: starting out from the well-known universality of the singular, he arrives at the singularity of the universal. He it was who exposed the crucial contradiction: every history is the whole of history; when the lightning flash that is man blazes out, all is said: all lives, all moments, all ages contingent miracles or misfires are *incarnations*: the Word becomes flesh, the universal establishes itself only by way of the living singularity that distorts it as it singularizes it. We should not see here a rehashing of the 'unhappy consciousness': it is precisely the opposite. Hegel is describing the tragic opposition between two abstract notions, the very ones that are, as I said, the two poles of our security. But, for Merleau, universality is never universal, except for 'soaring' thought: its birth is dependent on the flesh and, as flesh of our flesh, it retains, in its most subtle degree, our singularity. This is the admonition anthropology—be it analysis or Marxism—should not forget. Nor, should it forget, as Freudians do too often, that every man is the whole of man and that we must have regard in all human beings for the *lightning-flash,* that singular universalization of universality. Nor, as novice dialecticians do, should it be forgotten that the USSR is not the mere beginning of the universal revolution but also its incarnation, and that 1917 will bestow ineradicable features on future socialism. This is a difficult problem: neither banal anthropology nor historical materialism will free themselves from it. Merleau didn't think he was providing solutions. On the contrary, had he lived, he would have dug down even further into the problem, spiralling as ever, until he had radicalized the elements of the question, as we can see in 'Eye and Mind' from what he says of primordial historicity.[53] He did not reach the end of his thinking or, at least, he did not have time to express it in its entirety. Is this a failure? No, it is something like a taking-up of the initial contingency by the final contingency: singularized by this twofold absurdity and meditating upon singularity from the beginning to his death, Merleau's life takes on an inimitable 'style' and justifies by itself the warnings contained in the work. As for that work, which is inseparable from the life, a lightning flash between two chance events, lighting up our darkest night, we could apply to it, word for word, what he wrote at the beginning of this year:

> [I]f we cannot establish a hierarchy of civilizations or speak of progress—neither in painting nor in anything else that matters—it is not because some fate holds us back; it is, rather, because the very first painting in some sense

---

53 See Merleau-Ponty, 'Eye and Mind', *Primacy of Perception*, p. 161. [Trans.]

went to the farthest reach of the future. If no painting comes to be *the* painting, if no work is ever absolutely completed and done with, still each creation changes, alters, enlightens, deepens, confirms, exalts, re-creates or creates in advance all the others. If creations are not established advances, this is not only because, like all things, they pass away; it is also that they have almost all their lives still before them.[54]

As a question without an answer, a *virtú* without illusion, Merleau entered universal culture as something singular; he took his place as something universal in the singularity of history. Changing, as Hegel said, the contingent into the necessary and the necessary into the contingent, it was his mission to embody the problem of embodiment. On this question, we can all find a meeting place in his work.

I, who had other meetings with him, do not want to lie about our relations nor end on such fine optimism. I can still see his face that last night I saw him—we parted in the rue Claude-Bernard—a face disappointed, suddenly impenetrable. It remains with me, a painful wound, infected by regret, remorse and a little rancour. Transformed into what it will now be, our friendship is summed up in it for ever. Not that I accord the slightest privilege to the last moment, nor allot it the task of

---

54 See Merleau-Ponty, 'Eye and Mind', *Primacy of Perception*, p. 190 (translation modified).

telling the final truth about a life. But everything was, in fact, gathered in that face: frozen in that silent expression are all the silences he met me with after 1950, and at times, I, for my part, still feel the eternity of his absence as a deliberate mutism. I can clearly see that our final misunderstanding—which would have amounted to nothing if I could have seen him alive again—is cut from the same cloth as the others: it jeopardized nothing, and in it you can just see our mutual affection, our shared desire not to spoil anything between us. But you can see also the way our lives were out of phase, so that the initiatives we took were always out of kilter; and then, adversity intervening, it suspended our dealings, without violence, *sine die*. Like birth, death is an embodiment: his death, a nonsense full of obscure meaning, brought into being, where we were concerned, the contingency and necessity of an ill-starred friendship. Yet there was something there worth striving for: with our qualities and our shortcomings, the published violence of the one, the secret excesses of the other, we were not so badly suited. And what did we make of all that? Nothing, except that we avoided falling out. Everyone may apportion blame as they see fit: at any rate, we were not very guilty, so that sometimes I see in our adventure nothing but its necessity: this is how men live in our times; this is how they love each other: badly. That is true; but it is true also that it was we, we two, who loved each other badly. There are no conclusions to draw from this except that this long friendship—neither established nor undone, but simply wiped out at the point when it was either about to be reborn or break up—remains in me like an ever-open wound.

Les Temps modernes
(special issue, October 1961)

✳

A NOTE ON SOURCES

'Merleau-Ponty'

Originally published as 'Des rats et des hommes' in *Situations IV* (Paris: Gallimard, 1964), pp. 189–290.

First published in English translation in *Portraits* (London: Seagull Books, 2009), pp. 266–412.